CW00509790

grooves ....!
With love,
Cliè

RESISTANCE – The WHOLE TRUTH

By

Celia Jennings

Published in Great Britain 2009 by

MASTERWORKS INTERNATIONAL
27 Old Gloucester Street
London
WC1N 3XX
England

Tel: 00353 (0)86 325 2645
Email: info@mwipublishing.com
Web: http://www.mwipublishing.com

Copyright © 2009, Celia Jennings

ISBN: 0-9544450-7-4
13 digit ISBN: 978-0-954445-7-2

All rights reserved. No part of this book or other material may be reproduced in any form without written permission of the publishers.

Printed in the UK/USA by Lightning Source

RESISTANCE – The WHOLE TRUTH

By

Celia Jennings

CONTENTS

To all my teachers and all my relations
With eternal love and gratitude

Potential 'Quotes'

'This is Irresistible' – The Sun

'Very Arresting' – The Guardian

'Resistance is Futile' – The Leader

'La Pièce de Résistance' – Le Monde

'This Book is Awesome, Baby - my Resistance is low' - The Star

'Could be the start of a new Resistance Movement' - The Herald

'From Quantum Physics to DRAG Queens' - The Packet

'Join the Resistance Movement' - Sports Weekly

OVERVIEW

INTRODUCTION
PRO-LOGOS / FOREWORD / About the Author
A Limerick on Resistance and The 'Way of the Mule'
A: RESISTANCE in the OUTER, PHYSICAL WORLD

FOREWORD by Patricia Wylie

This unique book explores a topic, which may often be denied or avoided by those of us who are consciously on the "Spiritual Path." It is a book, which courageously explores the 'Upside' of a commonly acknowledged, 'downside' energy, *Resistance*. But then who decides what is downside in life and what is upside? As humans, we have the dark to know the light. And so it is with Resistance it seems.

Allow Celia to guide you to understanding, through this profound and timely book,Celia plays with you throughout her writing, a lovable characteristic of her true self in life. She humorously, and equally seriously, investigates Resistance from the viewpoint of the Scientist, Biologist, Metaphysician, Healer and Spiritualist in herself.

The first section will probably be relished by the thinkers and scientifically minded amongst you. Celia explores the Science of Resistance with an obvious knowledge and innate curiosity for her subject. If the Scientist/Biologist is dormant in you at the time of reaching for this booklet, go straight to Section B. The doorway will open to you reading Section A via starting in the middle. Celia won't mind, in fact you could start at the last page and read backwards and she would still be delighted. She understands these things and appreciates that the "right way" is **your** way.

If you are aware you have a Resistance to reading this book at all, then you will know it is for you. Being aware of Resistance offers an opportunity for change and the potential to unleash more life energy as she shows you with her understanding of the creation of electricity.

Celia has a unique and unusual way of understanding the world, the universe and such - so surrender, and allow her to take you down many winding paths. You will wonder at times where you are going to end up, but allow yourself an adventure and explore with her the myriad of physical and metaphysical deliberations she will engage you with. The journey could well be worth it, and your life changed immeasurably.

Blessings to all who seek the Divine, in allowing and growing through Resistance.

Patricia Wylie
Metaphysician, Humanitarian, Soul Dialoguer, Peace–Keeper of
Waitaha - Aotearoa, New Zealand

Acknowledgements

For Editing: My deepest thanks go to Patricia Wylie in New Zealand, and to Deborah and David Robinson in the UK, without whom, my text would be even more 'quirky' than it is. Additional grateful thanks go to David Lourie (see Dharma the Cat in websites at the end), for additional very helpful suggestions and insightful questions, most of which have been answered in this revised edition of April 2009
Celia (May 2009)

About the Author

Celia, born in London in 1953, is the grateful daughter of 2 amazing people: her mother Ingelore was German Jewish (hence the humour) and a strong humanitarian; her father Richard was a gentle Englishman, an artist with a deep connection to Spirit, a 'goonish' humour and a fascination for quantum physics.

Their separation when she was five, plunged her into her long journey of self discovery - through the intellectual study of Osteopathy, qualifying in 1977 from the BSO London progressing into so-called 'Cranial' Osteopathy, then into the exploration of experiential 'spirituality' from the age of 25; then in 1984 getting into general Humanistic Psychology, and more specifically into Breathwork, as her way to begin to purge her fears and self-doubts.

Her more physical journeys have taken her through many wonderful travels, connections with remarkable people, and visits with dolphins. All this has engendered in her a deep connection with Indigenous peoples, their earth-based culture, art and humour; world music, dance and cinema. She plays the fiddle, a 'flying-V' ukulele, and the 'bones', and currently lives in Bournemouth, Dorset, UK.

(Folk saying)   *Long did I resist and finally I gave way:*
The old person turns to dust, and the new one greets the day

Introduction

Everything in our known universe is subject to Resistance. It is the counter-force of all change in state. It is essential in all progress. This is understood in all physical processes, but as far as I can tell is not yet fully recognised as needed in the ever-expanding field of inner, or mental-emotional-spiritual process. My intention is to demonstrate that Resistance is a valuable and even essential part of change and growth, in every aspect of life.

This book was born in 2002 out of a recurring thought that grew louder in recent years. 'What's so bad about Resistance anyway? Why the bad press? It seems to be so popular, maybe there's a reason for it....'

It is said by some, that on approaching a new creative project, it is wise to 'keep it under your hat', for fear of weakening the purity of the project. I have not found this to be the case in this context. Instead, on mentioning the word 'Resistance' to my friends and clients, the response has been one of fascination and enthusiasm. Not only that, but most have voiced their own version of the observation that 'books on this subject are sorely needed.' Also, most people have given me fresh angles on the subject through the wording of their questions about it. For example, 'Resistance to what?', or 'are you helping people get in touch with their Resistance?' Then there were the many (in workshops, trainings and relationships) who pointed out how Resistant I was, and also how Resistant I must be to write about this ('You teach what you need to learn'). Well yes that's true, I admit to writing this book in my defence too. What else can I do with Saturn conjunct Mars in Scorpio?

So this is a book whose subtitle could be "RESISTANCE – A reference book for driving the Planet with the brakes on."

Actually, this is a book covering as many angles as I can perceive on the broad spectrum of Resistance. My fascination lies in the parallels between Physics and Metaphysics, the microcosm and the macrocosm, and I will endeavour to link these elements. This has almost become research on the subject, like a documentary, rather than a drama, wishing to encourage the reader to find their own thoughts on the matter. A thought-provoker, ideally.

Within our physical universe, the principle of Resistance is evident in many contexts. From the workings of electricity, and the fact that without a Resistor we wouldn't have toast - to showing the very necessary expression of political Resistance, without which we would not have social evolution. Resistance is worked with and overcome in physical Sports and therapies, in fact in every physical endeavour. And last, but not least, we also need to acknowledge its value in the process of our inner evolution, our personal and spiritual growth – the adversity that is the best and most thorough teacher.

This book is an exploration of this force that appears to be an impediment to our progress, but which is in fact vital to the success of all our endeavours. In other words, this book is 'waving the flag' for Resistance with the underlying statement: "Do not Resist your Resistance – it is telling you, or providing you with, something valuable." Resistance is not a 'mistake' that we make, or even an 'error' – it is too well-developed by our inner psyche. It is a means we have for creating safe boundaries, to make sure we don't go 'too far', too fast. It is a means of self-protection in a sometimes-hostile world.

I wish to show that not only is Resistance in itself not 'bad', but that it can be used as the **'slingshot of change'**, when it is made conscious.

Let us explore that.

Since my overall intention is to show the value of Resistance, and since I am personally fascinated by our world in all its magnificent outer and inner manifestations, I have chosen to cover every possible aspect of life in which Resistance occurs. For that reason, and for clarity, I have divided the book into 2 sections: One relating to the outer world and the other to the inner world.

Section A: RESISTANCE in the OUTER, PHYSICAL WORLD

Section B: RESISTANCE in the INNER, META-PHYSICAL WORLD: That is, those aspects of Resistance relating to the journey we all undertake, in our own individual ways, on the inner 'invisible' end of the spectrum of human existence.

Please gravitate to whichever section attracts you the most – but remember to explore the other too, at some point in time. You will have noticed by now that I am using a Capital R for each use of this word – this may be galling for the purists amongst us, but as my intention is to make conscious this fascinating principle, it is my way of drawing attention to the volume of reference there is available on the subject.

Please also accept the large number of quotes – so many people have written remarkable things. Not wishing to re-invent the wheel, I have chosen to quote their wisdom.

THE WAY OF THE MULE

Since the well-known characteristic of this unique animal is Resistance, he is well-placed for being the book's 'mascot.' In this revised edition, he weaves himself throughout the book, demonstrating how The Mule is unique because it is the result of the mating between a horse and a donkey – but is also sterile, so cannot reproduce itself.

This book tells the Tale of the Mule – for this is the *'Way of the Mule.'* It is dedicated to those of us who are reluctant to live or feel or do 'the right thing.' This reluctance may be due to fear of pain due to half-remembered consequences of past actions, or to fear of the future and its potential changes that bring with them huge responsibilities. However, it is also dedicated to those of us who are making genuine effort to become increasingly conscious in our thinking and in our actions.

The Mule is reluctant, or Resistant, but he always gets there in the end. *'The mule possesses the sobriety, patience, endurance and sure-footedness of the donkey and the vigour, strength and courage of the horse. Operators of working animals generally find mules preferable to horses: mules show less impatience under the pressure of heavy weights, and they show a natural resistance to disease and insects. Mules also exhibit a higher cognitive intelligence than their parent species - horses and donkeys. This is believed to be the result of hybrid vigour similar to how mules acquire greater height and endurance than either parents (donkey and horse).'* (Wikipedia)

'Mules are not really stubborn. They can seem lazy because they will not put themselves in danger. A horse can be worked until it drops, but not so with a mule. The "stubborn" streak is just the mule's way of telling humans that things are not right. Mules are very intelligent and it is not a good idea to abuse a mule. They will do their best for their owner, with the utmost patience.'

(From: http://www.lovelongears.com/about_mules.html)

For a short story with a happy ending, here is my Limerick:-
THE LIMERICK

There once was an ungrateful Mule
Whose purpose in life was to be cool
And yet his Resistance
Was met with persistence
From an Angel who loved this young fool

When we watch the young life of this Mule
We see that his home life was cruel
We know it's Ancestral
Since War was sequential
And societies live by this rule

But the life of our Mule was to change
As the Universe can rearrange
It was when his own violence
Was then met with kindness
While in prison doing 'time' with a Sage

The Sage would continue to ask
If the Mule would be up to the task
Of finding the Truth
In this half-equine youth
Who reluctantly peeled off his mask

But the heaven within was so brill
That our Mule began now to thrill
At the softness of Light
That now filled his sight -
He began to want to be still

When time came for our Mule to depart
And a new life was his now to start
He thence took the courage
To forgive the damage
And endeavoured to come from his heart

So, if ever you feel like a Mule
Remember the change in this fool
He chose not the masses
Of Asses and lasses,
But the way of the innermost jewel.

Section A:-
RESISTANCE in the OUTER, PHYSICAL WORLD
In this section, the Mule is a simple beast, subject to all the laws of 3D life.

Chapter 1 – 'In the beginning was the Word'

Of: The Beginning of all things,
The Big Bang, Black Holes and giraffes

> *'In the beginning was the Word, and the Word was with God and the Word was God' (John 1:1)*
> *Crisis (Catastrophe) is Opportunity Chinese Proverb*
> *Resistance Acknowledged is Opportunity   CCJ*

In every act of Creation from the greatest to the smallest, Resistance is an essential obstacle that needs to be overcome or co-operated with, in order to create something that can work and grow. Any act of creation would be impossible without the force that exists to oppose that change of state.

This is how we begin our exploration, and this is how it all began. That is, the Universe/s are understood by some to have been initiated in this way: *The Word*, which was perhaps a deep sound or vibration, was hummed out at the Dawn of Time in one huge creative moment. The Big Bang, which is estimated to have occurred 13.6 billion years ago, could also be seen as God's decision to manifest as matter. Whether you believe God created the Universe, or the Big Bang did, it is worth asking why these are contradictory, and what is God anyway? The point is that the Universe has been expanding for millennia (surprisingly the most concise and full details of our position and velocity come from the Monty Python Galaxy song), but the acceleration of this process is diminishing

Science or religion, it was truly a matter of magic and mastery in the highest sense. With the release of the energy held within that Black Hole (could this have been the 'un-manifest void'?) Light flooded the newly-created space, manifesting at the visible and invisible ends of the spectrum. Our planet, flung out we may say from this centre, began its journey of boiling, cooling and stirring its primordial soup. The resultant microscopic creatures that developed into plants, animals and then us, have had a fundamental urge to transform. This urge has been far greater than any Resistance to change. Yet the very force that Resists change is also essential in all progress.

RESISTANCE in NATURE

The nature of this Resistance has been the overcoming of obstacles - such as how to reach those delicious-smelling, life-saving leaves high up in the trees, for the short-necked-giraffes in the making. The Resistance generated by Gravity is a major force that has to be overcome and worked with – so the giraffe neck in this case had to be strong and stable, and counterbalanced by the rest of the body, like a crane. Perhaps the short-necked giraffes that were reluctant to stretch could be called 'lazy' or Resistant! Since necessity is the 'mother of invention', this is how Natural Selection probably worked its magic to produce our wonderful and seemingly boundless array of life forms. However, when we talk about the human brain, it is now being shown to develop in evolutionary leaps, rather than doing so steadily. We may also choose to perceive this process as being the way God set it up to work. It could just be a matter of choice and opinion. Why did it all begin? We can only conjecture in an anthropomorphising sort of way, that there was a need or desire for God him/herself to experience 'itself' - to create a mirror that would reflect every aspect of its' Being. To continue this conjecture, did the greatest power that is, Resist this change in his / her evolution (seeming unnecessary from our finite viewpoint), until the tension between the need for change and the comfort of being the Lord of whatever there was before that, became too great, and resolve itself into the 'Big Bang'?

THE BIG BANG

From the understanding given by our current physicists, especially by Stephen Hawking, this is one way we can perceive that moment of the birth of Universes. It looks as if the Big Bang erupted from the almost infinite compression of a Black Hole into a tiny speck, - and a moment of *Singularity of Infinite Gravity* (Michio Kaku) on its *event horizon* – resulting in that surprising Galactic Mother of fire and brimstone, the basic stuff of Creation. But what was it that existed before that moment of super-compression that would be drawn into itself, and its womb of All Possibilities?

Maybe God and science are not separate – maybe all the Strings, Gluons, Quarks, Particles and undulating Light waves are manifestations of that Ultimate Intelligence some call God. Possibly the only reason to avoid calling it 'God', is the huge mental-emotional charge we humans place on the God of our very limited understanding. Yet 'God' is an excellent name to give to an ultimate intelligence whose creation and universal laws we are endlessly discovering, and to which can be ascribed the qualities of **G**enerator, **O**perator/Organiser, and **D**estroyer.

Chapter 2 – It's Electrifying and it's Magnetising!

Of: Electrifying matters, Flint-knapping, Attraction
Primordial Soup & Resistance Capacitors

*'There is no thing that is endowed with life - from man, who is
enslaving the elements, to the nimblest creature - in all this world,
that does not sway in its turn. Whenever action is born from force,
though it be infinitesimal, the cosmic balance is upset and
universal motion results'* (Tesla 1925)

*The objecting students are Re-Volting again
A Resistor normally opens when it burns out
'Watt, no Ohm to go to ?'*

Kilroy-Foo the Resistor

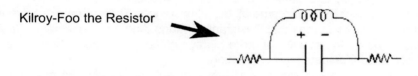

Electrical Resistance is the phenomenon by which electrical energy flow is slowed down to create heat, as the flow is impeded by a change of wire thickness or the material used in the circuit, or by giving it a much longer distance to travel. This heat production has resulted in, among other things, some of our favourite inventions, such as the ubiquitous toaster and the marvellous bar-heater. It can be likened to the flow of water through a pipe, where the Resistance would be the tap itself, slowing down the speed and quantity of water allowed to flow.

It is interesting how Time is an important factor in this heat-producing result. The speed of the propagated impulse is a factor of the distance travelled, plus the time taken to move that distance. But, if electrical motion without the passage of time were actually possible, then Resistance would have no place in our Universe. This is because the impulse has to travel a certain distance within a certain time-frame, and the lower the Resistance, the easier and faster the progress of the impulse. Less Resistance would of course result in no heat production either, and all the uses we make of that. So then, without Resistance we wouldn't have heat – we would be cold. This principle of the use of Resistance goes back to the days of flint-knapping and fire-making. Imagine trying to create a spark without the Resistance of the flint that you are striking – the stone would be smooth and the sliding motion would not allow a spark - there would be no friction, and no fire. We would not be here, in this state of evolution. The passage of electricity, in a form useful to mankind, would not be possible without Resistance. It would simply and quickly be absorbed by the ground.

LIGHTNING BIRTH

The world of electricity, the flow of energy along its path of least Resistance, remains fascinating to the observer. Made visible by the old-fashioned Van de Graaff generators, a sense of magic and awe accompanies the crackle and hum of unpredictable but controlled forks of light. What mysterious act of creation is being unleashed, threatening our sense of normality? With the release of nitrogen from the atmosphere during those early lightning storms of swirling gases and raindrops, complex compounds could coalesce and co-create our living matter.

Reaching back in time to the birth of our planet, what were the sources of Resistance that could make the chance of life beginning, very slim? There were only simple, inorganic chemical compounds in the atmosphere and on primeval land. Yet the very chaos that ruled, by supposed chance collision of simple elements, and electrical discharge, combined to set off chain-reactions that, billions of years later, have brought us here.

The Resistance to this process occurred in the form of constant change, intense wind, heat, atmospheric chaos, and a young and rootless soil. Yet, what was the ingredient that overcame all this Resistance? Time - that extra dimension that changes all, even the most Resistant of things. And yet, those same Resistant influences forced the making of more highly nutritious soil, into which roots could cling, and build life-sustaining vegetation.

Since this prehistoric and violent atmospheric activity, we now only have occasional reminders of our chaotic past, in the form of thunder and lightning storms. And yet Benjamin Franklin in 1752 courageously harnessed the storm's strength in his famous key experiments - he was certain, from his observations, that the electrical impulse would be attracted to the metal of the key on the end of his string, then travel down the string to hit the ground, where it would disperse and be absorbed, safely earthed. Our electrical revolution had such humble beginnings – clearly we have developed so a world of technologically since then.

It has since been noted that electricity travels at different (slow) speeds and that the electrons of a Direct Current do not move strictly like a current in a river; while a propagated electromagnetic wave moves at almost the speed of light. Nevertheless the flow is directly affected by various forms of Resistance, from the conductivity of the wire, to its length and thickness, and the receptivity of the engine. The very inter-relationship of electricity and magnetism in motion (using a Resistance capacitor, polarised or not, to store electricity for a short time) is the basis of our current (pun intended) global communications and travel.

As we search for the most efficient materials for tasks we need to resolve, either working with or against Resistance, we become increasingly inventive about the effects on our environment. We can also be more conscious of the upset balance of nature, created by our over-use or abuse of the Planet's resources.

MAGNETIC FORCES

The spin of electrons around its nucleus creates a magnetic force, to a greater or lesser extent in every material. In addition, when *'many of the electron spins are aligned in the same direction, they act cooperatively, creating a net magnetic field'* (Wikipedia). This situation occurs in a bar magnet, with its familiar effects on iron filings scattered in its force field.

Magnetism and electricity are fundamentally interlinked, and one cannot be studied without witnessing the effects of the other.

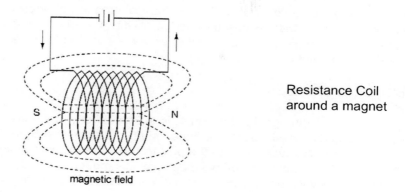

Resistance Coil around a magnet

magnetic field

However, the force of magnetism is greater when particles are in motion, as they are in a current, whether they are vibrating in the AC current 'shimmy' or in the DC current's slow advance, as if through thick porridge. They are so interconnected that the two forces are referred to in quantum physics as an electro-magnetic field.

POWER STATIONS

In our rush to create 'bigger and better' everything, using increasing amounts of electricity, we have invented nuclear power. Sadly this is not historically correct in the sense that it was not the initial motivation for splitting the atom, but now we have nuclear power stations, and need to look to the future regarding their use and abuse. The seemingly 'free' source of energy has hidden costs, which lie in the long-term consequences of nuclear energy production. The actual costs of de-commissioning an out-of-date or failing nuclear power station, where the active ingredients and waste products must be safely disposed of, are astronomical. And of course the land on which it stands, will no longer be available for use by any other industry for thousands of years to come, because of the very slow 'half-life' process of radio-active decay. However, for now it is the 'cleanest' option, in terms of carbon dioxide production.

The need to address these failings may in the future drive us to create more eco-friendly forms of power-generation. We have become too dependent on outside sources for our daily comforts and joys – too certain of the light-switch and functioning sockets – to go without these functions. However, looking at power and agriculture, without electricity and our large populations, (and the dominance of certain chosen seed banks) the older more naturally resilient / Resistant seed banks would probably re-assert themselves, since nature is always the winner in the game of Time.

The MULE as POWER STATION

On a lighter note, given the reluctant nature of our beast of burden, it would be safe to assume its relief at the mechanical creation of energy – our way to harness electricity without muscular work. Until the industrial revolution, one turn of the winch was equivalent to one unit of power – that is many miles and hours of walking round and round.

BUILDING BRIDGES

Moving through this Section A, in the 'outer' physical universe, I am also building bridges occasionally to the 'inner' worlds, to show how connected they are.

The cross-over between the physical and the Metaphysical is aided and abetted by the use of common words across this great (apparent) divide. Look at how seamlessly we use these words and phrases (probably used mostly in other languages as well):

(where E is electrical, and P is for an aspect of physics & astronomy):

E Needing to be Earthed
E Having your wires crossed
E Blowing a fuse
E 'The power you're supplying – it's electrifying !' ('Grease') !
E Amplifying the situation
E Negativity & positivity
E Wired for sound / feeling wired (think of coffee)
P Magnetism between them / poles apart / coming into your orbit
P Light-years away
P Gravity of the situation

There are of course many more examples, but the use of language is fascinating and very powerful in every context, and can help us recharge our batteries, when we enjoy this connection.

So, Resistance is not only extremely valuable in the world of electricity, it is also essential in the world as we know it. If we are to have our cake, bake it, and eat it, that is.

Chapter 3 – Science and Omni-Science

Of: Quantum Matter, Time, Space, Gravity, Light & Inertia
Galileo, Superstring, Glue, Multiverses and Dimensions
This Binary Universe, Darwin and bunnies

> Einstein: *"God does not play at dice with the Universe"*
> Nils Bohr: *"Albert, stop telling God what to do"*
> *Energy cannot be created or destroyed – it can only change form*
> *'Even in your world … (a flaming ball of gas) is not what a star is, but only what it is made of'*   CS Lewis – *'Voyage of the Dawn Treader'*
> *Life is a D.R.A.G. – it is full of Density, Resistance,*
> *Adversity and Gravity … until you fly*   CCJ

The world of Science and Nature is full of wonder, and as such is a taste of the Divine when it engenders enthusiasm ('entheos' Greek, 'in god" – as an expression of godly passion). and excitement in those who discover its laws

In this chapter, I wish to explore some of the different laws and sciences of our planet and the universe as we know it, to show how and where Resistance operates. These sciences are generally studied separately as Physics or Chemistry or in sub-groups.

Ever since Galileo (1564-1642) questioned long-held theories or beliefs that had put the Earth in the centre of the universe, the division between science and religion has grown immense. And yet this antagonistic connection appears to be turning full-circle. More and more evidence seems to be gathering to show intelligence behind the laws governing our universe – an intelligence some prefer to call God.

However, for reasons given in Chapter 1, it would be better to keep the 2 worlds apparently apart, to allow clear examination of the evidence. Then those of us who love to see the connection between these two worlds of science, or the finite, and the Divinity of the infinite, can enjoy the parallels as they are proven.

GRAVITY

Galileo concurred with the Polish Copernicus, who wrote in 1543 that the movements of the planets were 'helio-centric', or sun-centred. The Italian is well-renowned for his : *"..lifelong struggle to free scientific inquiry from restriction by philosophical and theological interference."* (Encarta).

He is also credited with having changed the course of physics to it being founded on *"precise measurements rather than on metaphysical principles and formal logic."*

Galileo's own Resistance to the rigidly held ideas of the faithful of his time, heralded the start of modern science as we know it. It was the end of the co-dependence of science with religious authority – science was able to start 'growing up' and investigate the world afresh. He held that *"Interpretation of the Bible should be adapted to increasing knowledge and that no scientific position should ever be made an article of Roman Catholic faith."*

His own field of interest lay mostly in Astronomy. But he was also famed for his demonstration that falling bodies are subject to gravity at the same rate of fall, whatever their weight (landing-times depending on the air Resistance to that body) – which he tested from the top of the leaning Tower of Pisa. He proved that a falling body, of any size, cannot Resist the effect of gravity.

Herein lay the gravity of his situation, since he opposed the religious thinking of his time,. The universe was seen as being 'terra-centric' that all planetary motion occurred around the Earth. He was tried and convicted as a heretic and spent the last 2 years of his life under house arrest.

Galileo also made an unsuccessful attempt to measure the speed of light from one hilltop to another, in the early 1600's. It is not surprising that he failed at that time, considering the actual speed of light.

The most famous name in connection with the observation of gravity is Sir Isaac Newton. The arrival of the apple on his head that fateful day, jolted his awareness, and may also have aided his logical abilities. He was able to present 3 fundamental laws of physics in 1687, which formed the basis of physics until the early 1900's, and are still used today.

INERTIA, DRAG and ENTROPY

Inertia is the Resistance that an object has to a change in order to alter it's state of motion. Newton's definition of inertia is that:-
'.. the innate force of matter is a power of resisting, by which every body, as much as in it lies, endeavors to preserve in its present state, whether it be of rest, or of moving …forward.' In other words all things have a tendency to Resist change. If it wasn't for friction affecting moving objects, or gravity dragging on objects at rest, those objects would remain either in their trajectory or at rest.

The purpose of inertia is to conserve energy, by attempting to maintain equilibrium. However, long-term equilibrium is in effect unattainable, since everything is in a dynamic state of change by nature. This motion, or lack of motion, is best measured against other objects that appear to move the least, such as the stars.

Einstein proved that energy and mass are interchangeable, His Special Theory of Relativity shows that if mass (matter) exhibits the principle of inertia (keeping its current state of motion or lack of it), then inertia must also apply to energy as well.

According to Isaac Asimov in "Understanding Physics": "this tendency for motion (or for rest) to maintain itself steadily, unless made to do otherwise by some interfering force, can be viewed as a kind of "laziness," a kind of unwillingness to make a change' (Wikipedia on Inertia).

In fluid or aerodynamics, *Drag* which is sometimes called Resistance, is the force that Resists the movement of a solid object through the medium of liquid or gas. The forces are friction or pressure, which drag and slow down the object's motion, which in a powered vehicle is overcome by thrust (Wikipedia).

On a lighter note, perhaps the best way to overcome Inertia would be with the thrust of a rocket, which would result in some very spectacular 'drag-racing.'

Once change is in process, the 2nd law of thermodynamics comes into operation, showing how the tendency of all things is towards *entropy* (which is measurable through temperature change over Time) or disorder. Another way of putting this is that the highest probability of outcome is that Nature will always takes over sooner or later – whether by dust, 'pests', 'overgrowth', or alteration by the elements through the weather. Yet there is order in this seeming chaos.

In the LIGHT of THOUGHT

It was to take another 200 years or so after Galileo, before the speed of Light was accurately measured as being about 186,000,000 miles per second. Light itself demonstrates interesting qualities. The Greeks contemplated light, initially declaring that light issued forth from objects, including the eye itself (Pythagorus and Plato in the 5th Century BC). However it was a little-known Egyptian, named Alahazen, who disproved this 5 centuries later. Aristotle was aware of the refractory property of light in rainbows in his day, and the Dutch theorist Snell mathematically explained it, in 1620.

The scientist Rene Descartes (1596-1650) also experimented with optics and the laws of reflection, as well as conducting other studies in geometry and algebra. But he is most well-known today as 'the father of modern philosophy.' He wanted to apply mathematical precision to a view of the order of life, and he is most well-known for his statement:

"Cogito, ergo sum"…I think, therefore I am…From his postulate that a clear consciousness of his thinking proved his own existence, he argued the existence of God, who, according to Descartes' philosophy, created two classes of substance that make up the whole of reality. One class was thinking substances, or the minds', and the other was extended substances, or bodies. He concluded that: 'reason was the only reliable method of attaining knowledge' (Encarta).

The unforeseen consequences of this philosophy have been enormous, in ways outlined below, which many would argue, has never been 'a bad thing.' However, an increasing number of people are of the opinion that this 'Cartesian' (meaning: 'of Descartes') view of the world, has resulted in a huge split in our understanding of humanity. The Cartesian view asserts that the mind and body are separate, and do not inter-relate. His thinking was his own, but of course would not have been anticipated by him to have such far-reaching effects on thought since his day. The consequences have resulted in the following modern situations concerning our physical and mental health:

Over-full hospitals: Where the body is seen as the only source of disease (and not really stress for instance) and where only physical treatments are advocated;

Nutritional fatigue:	Where supplements fabricated in laboratories are considered to be good nutritionally, even though they may be 'life-less', because it cannot be proven by (currently) measurable means, that 'life' is an important co-factor in good nutrition;
Psychiatry:	The study of the 'ghost in the machine' – which is how the mind was seen by Descartes, as summarised by Gilbert Ryle in 1949;
Mental fatigue:	The search for meaning in our times, leads many to seek solace or something greater, in drugs legal or illegal, without emotional guidance;

Short-term thinking in all spheres of action: - If we don't believe mind and body to be interwoven, then we are likely to act only for today.

THOUGHT on LIGHT

Meanwhile, in the 'light of' the history of the understanding of light….Einstein showed that: " the speed of light has to remain constant, and all the rest of physics had to be changed to be consistent with this fact. This Special Theory of Relativity was to have many unexpected physical consequences…"

One of these was the formula that is universally known, and has been linked forever with the completion of the atom bomb : e = mc2 (where c is the known constant of the speed of light). This formula shows that energy and matter potentially become equal at the speed of light (squared). In other words, if an object could travel at the speed of light, it would lose its properties of solid matter, and simply become energy as light. He continued to show mathematically that Time itself would also slow down to zero movement – imagining that sending a clock travelling into the speed of light, the analogue hands would slow down and finally stop moving, relative to objects moving at less than the speed of light.

Albert Einstein postulated, (based on Planck's quantum hypothesis) that light itself consists of individual quanta. These later came to be called photons (1926). *'From Einstein's simple postulation was borne a flurry of debating, theorizing and testing, and thus, the entire field of 'quantum physics' was born (Wikipedia – photons)*

QUANTUM PHYSICS

Further developments in our understanding of light have resulted in the Quantum physics we know and love, or at least we would like to appear to understand, so well.

As more was discovered about our Universe in the early part of the 20th century, it was seen that if Newtonian mechanics governed the workings of an atom, electrons would rapidly travel towards, and collide with, the nucleus. However, in the natural world, the electrons normally remain in an unknown orbital path around the nucleus, defying classical electromagnetism. It became clear that a whole new way of explaining the workings of our space-time continuum had to be considered.

The most well-known names in connection with this evolution in thought, are Max Planck, Albert Einstein, Niels Bohr, David Bohm, Erwin Schrödinger, and many others

With our increasing knowledge of Quantum Electro-magnetics (QE), has come the awareness of the essential nature of Vibration. The *String Theory*, which was gathering momentum in the early 1980's, under the devoted gaze of John Schwarz and Michael Green in particular, has come to explain many of the aspects of so-called 'strong and weak forces' that operate in the Universe. These include explanations of gravity at work in the Black Holes themselves, and at great distances from them too.

Lynne McTaggart in her book 'The Field', has researched and summarised this subject in depth, especially its repercussions for us in everyday life.

VIBRATING STRINGS

The *String Theory* speaks of how all subatomic particles are tiny vibrating strings that have higher dimensions of space trapped inside them. They only appear to be different particles because of the different ways they vibrate, creating a giant mesh of vibrating strings. To Einstein, their movement would still be seen to be bending, when monitored over large expanses of space, and to the Quantum physicist, these particles would seem wavy and fuzzy, like vibrating musical strings are, when looked at closely.

Each vibration of a string corresponds to a Particle – this is a Quantum (packet). The 'strings' also exist in our 'Multiverse' of *Parallel Universes*, and are not confined to one space or time. They are also reflected in their *anti-matter* versions, like negative moving pictures of the same image and event. A now famous idea to explain this, was put forward by Schrodinger, using the idea of putting his cat in a box, which would have a poison released (thankfully not carried out). He theorised that the cat would be dead in this universe or dimension, but alive in another, and simultaneously too, although 'entangled' by being inter-connected with its counterpart.

What we perceive of as solid matter, is actually mostly space. The huge distances between the atomic particles and their nuclei, are relatively so vast that space is by far the largest component. And as we are speaking of the foundational structures of everything we know, all matter, no matter how solid it appears, mainly consists of space. But when we think of 'space' we naturally think of a vacuum, which should be inert.

However, it has been proved that space actually has its own 'force' that can affect other structures. This substance that makes up the huge apparent vacuum of Space, is termed *dark matter and dark energy, or quintessence*.

The most momentous discovery by quantum science, that has repercussions in all areas of our lives, especially concerning research itself, has been the discovery that the presence of an observer and his expectations, affect the outcome of an experiment. It appears that electrons are spread out randomly (how this is ascertained is hard to comprehend), until a conscious observer decides to look at them. This has huge implications for all experiments, as well as all other aspects of life. The anticipated outcome of the experiment is referred to as its' 'Probability.' To take this to its largest and most mind-shaking conclusion – we must (at least) be co-creating our entire Universe.

PHOTONS & DOPPELGANGERS

Wave-Particle Duality was first measured in the early quantum experiments. It was observed that 2 light beams that were shone through 2 slits, were not simply landing on the opposite screen in 2 areas as expected – but in 3 areas. The way this was understood was that some of the photons of light split and reconnected round the slits in the board, meeting in the middle.

So there is a *Probability* that one electron can hit more than one place at any one time, since water, sound, light and particles, all have wave-like properties, and can spread out and exist in or affect more than one place at any one time. This would also explain the unpredictability of particles, which are seen as behaving like people who may or may not behave predictably.

When this capacity of a light wave to split in two was observed, it led to huge and ongoing explorations into the nature of, and indeed the illusion of, reality.

RESISTANCE AS THE NECESSARY DOPPELGANGER

This may be the ideal place in which to introduce the notion that Resistance could be the *'anti-matter'* of evolution. In the world of evolution and change, Resistance could be seen as the reflected image as if it were a 'tennis partner' playing opposite the 'player-of-Least-Resistance' - the essential co-player, whose input creates a true game, the game of life.

The HOLOGRAPHIC UNIVERSE

A hologram is a picture copy with exact replication of its source that can be split into a myriad of pieces. Each of these fragments still shows the full scope of the original, although detail is less defined in the tiniest fragments

The process of creating a hologram can also be applied to a moving picture. Holograms themselves can be reproduced at a distance from their source – as popularised in the movie *'Star Wars'* (the very first film of the trilogy) when the holographic image of Princess Leia is projected for Obi-wan Kenobi by the robot R2D2. The Holographic Universe (see Talbot) is reflected in the holographic nature of our brains.

Karl Pribram, in his brain and memory research written in 1968, shaped his theory of how the brain operates, into an understanding that it does so as a Hologram of itself. So every part of the brain can be aware of what any other part of the brain is involved with, concurrently. This understanding can be applied to the whole body, through its' instant response in related places, to a shock or a memory of a shock, for example. He termed this the 'physiology of remembering', stating that: "Memory is reconstructive rather than reduplicative.'

Because of this, it led Dr. Gerald Edelman (in Chopra) to hold that *'no one literally repeats a memory; (there is) always something different about it ,'such as perhaps the context, or the emotions connected with the event. 'Memory is a creative act then, ...(and) every experience one has in life changes the brain's anatomy.'* Talbot expanded this notion into one that explains *'The brain is a hologram enfolded in a holographic universe'* (expanding on Bohm and Pribram).

OUR COMPUTER-WORLD

The workings of the universe are now being likened to the workings of a computer (reported by Braden). The now-complex computer is still programmed and run by a system of 'yes-no' commands – the binary system. Even though an 'on-off' system of mathematics was being explored in India and in Egypt centuries ago, the modern version began to be developed in its current format in the early 1940's. It seems we might be living in our own *virtual reality*. Could this be the 'illusion' alluded to by the ancient religions?

Resistance could be the 'off' for the 'on' of the *binary* computer language, the 'no' for the 'yes' of our Dualistic Quantum Universe.

WATER

In his beautiful work photographing defrosting water crystals, at electron microscope levels, Maseru Emoto has shown very graphically how thought can have a very powerful effect on this substance. Nobody else has been able to reproduce his experimental results though – but when asked why, he replied (at the Breath of Life Conference London 2007) that it must have something to do with his own child-like quality! Nevertheless, his results are photographic, and all so very different that they could not possibly be manipulated by clever computer use. Each word or thought projected verbally or mentally onto the defrosting water, by any observer/s, has its own pattern that is visible in these exquisite photos. It would be interesting to see the effects that the word 'Resistance' might have on these crystals…

The power of this work lies in the fact that, as our bodies are made up of 70% water (as well as being mostly space that is!), every thought and word that we utter and think, and that we submerse ourselves in, has an effect on the actual structure and function of our bodies both immediately, and over time.

POPULAR QUANTUM SCIENCE

Through Quantum physics, science has entered the world of 'popular science', as its explanations continue to support an increasing understanding of life at deeper levels. These areas can be summarised as:
1.   The Interconnectedness of all things, through time and space;

2. Space, Time and Matter are all made of the same subatomic substance, much as water, ice & steam are the same substance in different states;
3. All of material creation may be said to be conscious;
4. Science fiction' is showing itself to be far closer to 'science fact' than we would previously admit – for example, wormholes and parallel universes and other dimensions (10 dimensions have been mathematically figured out so far), and the implications for time travel;
5. Superstring connecting other dimensions, Quantum non-locality showing that no atom can be anticipated to be in any one place at any one time – it is in every place all at once;
6. Electromagnetics and Vibrational frequencies across the spectrum of light, are seen as being at the core of our consciousness-raising, giving awareness and intention for 'Ascension' for the increasing number of 'Lightworkers';
7. 'All life, coexisting together at the same time, is both matter and space: movement and stillness, sound and silence, light and darkness' ('starstuffs.com');
8. Shamanic, and possibly some magicians' manipulation of objects in the 4th Dimension' may now be partially explained in this way;
9. Jung's Synchronicity and the Collective Unconscious, may be explained by means of the String Theory of interconnectedness;
10. Emotion – feeling is the fuel of creation: it's passion is what empowers our thought into manifestation; this emotion is energised by association and experience in the holographic brain-universe;
11. Prayer – affirms our Oneness, and adds trusting emotional energy to our wishes, making them more easily created ;
12. A Paradigm SHIFT is happening now;
13. Is death the end, or a beginning of change into another dimension?

QUANTUM RESISTANCE

This word 'Quantum' has reached far into our consciousness, and into many unexpected areas of our lives. It is as if the very depth and width of the subject has captured imaginations everywhere. There are now so many contexts within which Quantum thinking has been integrated. This may or may not infuriate real Quantum physicists – it would be wonderful to feel that they, in general, feel included in the wider world, rather than cloistered away in the world of their extra-ordinary thoughts.

Some terms that have undulated their way into our almost daily vocabulary, and filled our fascinating virtual space, are the following:

Quantum Web   the Inter-connectedness of all things (String theory)

Quantum Healing   *'Research on spontaneous cures of cancer, conducted (how? Author's note) in both the US and Japan, has shown that just before the cure appears, almost every patient experiences a dramatic shift in awareness....such patients jump to a new level of consciousness that prohibits the existence of cancer. Then the cancer cells either disappear, literally overnight in some cases, or at the very least stabilize without damaging the body any further. (This) sudden change...denotes a discrete jump from one level of functioning to a higher level —a quantum leap'* (Chopra – p.17). Certainly spontaneous and sudden absence of cancer has been witnessed in for example, people with multiple personality disorder, where one personality has a cancer, and the others do not.

Quantum Leap   *'is a change of an electron from one energy state to another within an atom. It is discontinuous; the electron jumps from one energy level to another instantaneously'* (Wikipedia) This expression is also used to describe great change that occurs in someone's life circumstances or their thinking.

Quantum Leap-frogging   (OK this is my phrase, for helping each other into greater consciousness)

Quantum Booster   An energy-healing device, similar to Rife or Vega diagnostic machines

Quantum Chaos   (Beyond me)

Quantum spaghetti   (According to a Matt Baier's quirky website) *'Continuing towards the core of the black hole, for you have no choice, you will then become Quantum Spaghetti. This is quantum foam after all the molecules have broken down and the atoms rearranged. It looks rather like quantum foam, only stretched into long, thin strands. It also tastes marginally better than quantum foam.'*

Quantum Mysteries   *'light going through a "double slit" experiment seems to know before it sets out in its journey, exactly what kind of 'traps' have been set for it along the way'* Which looks like the beginning of even more amazing discoveries – see www.lifesci.sussex.ac.uk

Quantum Shift TV   *'We tell stories to inspire positive action'* (local and global)

Quantum Entanglement   This describes where *'2 or more objects are linked together so that one object can no longer be adequately described without full mention of its counterpart – even though the objects may be spatially separate'* (Wikipedia)

Quantum Evolution   *'shows how the quantum multiverse rather than God or creationism accounts for the origin of life and evolution'* – (Johnjoe McFadden's own website)

Quantum Teleportation   Useful for communication

'Quantum of Solace'   - would you believe it, James Bond is now hot on the trail in a new film for this 'adventurer' !!!

Quantum Communication   (Its' physics is beyond me)

Quantum Lottery   - as explored by Southampton University – we are all winners somewhere in the multiverse! Now that's fair! Looking at the curriculum for the 2008 Oxford University Conference on

'Quantum Interaction' we see an amazing array of topics covered, as outlined in their website:

Quantum Mechanics *(QM) is emerging from physics into non quantum domains such as human language, cognition, information retrieval, biology, political science, economics, organizations, and social interaction. The organizers of the Second Quantum Interaction Symposium are interested in advancing and applying the methods and structures of QM to these and other non-quantum domains.*

Since OU is where Stephen Hawking resides, we might safely say that he does enjoy the wide panoply of applications of his favourite topic.

And finally, the

Quantum Bandwagon - The one that only the best people ride on;

So, 'Quantum Resistance' might be Resistance requiring gravity to work thoroughly?

MULISH SCIENCE

Let us give this weird and wonder-ful science a context of understanding for the now-famed Mule, travelling as indeed we are, in space and time. Imagine he can be seen in all the dimensions that can be strung together, and all his Quantum packets of light have coalesced as he hurtles through space and time. We see that his atomic structure, as is all matter, is made up of 99% space. Could it be that Muffin is made of Nuffin? Well nearly.

Yet his hairy light-body is subject to all the strong and weak gravity-like forces of the universe, while the strongest influence on him is the force of inertia. However, in his own parallel universe, he has all the opposite characteristics: he is keen and determined, strong and enthusiastic, wild and free. Our odd-toed ungulate will meet himself coming round in the opposite direction one day, and be very inspired.

BUNNIES

Perhaps the last word on evolutionary science can go to the humble bunny-rabbit:-

"Side by side with the bones of the sabre-tooth tiger were remains of the harmless bunny-rabbit. Many individual rabbits must have been killed and eaten by the tiger and other predators without offering any Resistance; but the curious fact is that the rabbit population has survived and increased, whereas the sabre-tooth tiger is an extinct species. "Blessed are the meek, for they shall inherit the earth."
#38 in the Swedenborg Digital Library

Could it be that the Bunny demonstrates Resistance-by-numbers? This would be the case, when we look at the results of the horrors we have thrown at this gentle creature. Certainly, it would seem that, in this context, the *non-Resistant* shall inherit the Earth. Although that argument is flawed too – witness the humble cockroach, whose perpetual Resistance in the face of mass extinction seems to manifest in the form of sheer ignorance. Perhaps if the dinosaurs had adapted according to this cartoon, things might have been very different!

With thanks to Simon Drew, at www.simondrew.co.uk

Chapter 4 –Religion, New Age and Resistance

Of: G.O.D, Beliefs and Truth, Dinosaurs,
Philosophy, Descartes, Duality
New Age Metaphysics;

*"There is no point in fighting with someone's beliefs - you can't, they
are invisible... Instead, I prefer to engage with the heart –
the hope-maker, the lover of Life.
That's where I want to focus my attention."*
Prem Rawat (also known by the title Maharaji)
'The only religion is humanity' Herakhan Babaji

Religion can be defined as a belief system centred around a Divine and mystical power greater than ourselves, a power that is Omni-present, Omni-potent, and Omni-scient. However it is also linked with dogmatism, tradition, scholarly pursuits, and those who have been prepared to die (and kill) for their beliefs, and those who have been Resistant or have adapted to colonisers' belief-systems.

A HISTORY of RELIGION

Since the dawn of Time, for most of humankind, and especially for Indigenous and traditional cultures, religion has been the lore of Mother Earth, the flow and weaving of the land through human veins. The anthropomorphism of deities has been a means of teaching the principles and laws of nature, to garner respect for her power, and enable people to work in cooperation with it.

There have always been stories ranging from inspired leaders, or at the other end of the enlightenment perspective, the jealous pursuit of earthly and spiritual power within a clan. Spiritual leaders have traditionally had as much, and sometimes more, power than worldly leaders, so this conflict is fairly inevitable.

The Resistance in this context lies within the struggle for power, and the associated battles that have peppered the history of mankind.

Meanwhile a quiet spiritual revolution and evolution has been happening for others. Almost every religion seems to have been inspired by the wisdom of a single human being that has realised (made real) their core-connection with the Source. However, more careful examination of the early days of any of those religions shows that the Master himself has not (usually) been the direct author of it.

It was created and written down, sometimes long after his death (except in the case of Mohammed), as a man-made method of propagation, and of control of the semi-understood teachings; a means of retaining power.

Traditionally the new teachings, and the devotion of the followers, have often been 'too much' for the incumbent religion of the day. The Resistance to hearing the truth has resulted in persecution of the Master or some of the devotees who chose to stay with their Teacher, because of the joy they experienced in the Knowledge and in his presence and teachings. They may even have lived in times when it was felt necessary to die for their beliefs, for their faith and their experience.

Witness the very early Christians or some of the saints, well-known through accounts of the strength of faith in their God. This God of the many Saints in every religion, may have been named Jehovah or Allah, Shiva, Krishna, or the 'no-god' of Buddhists, or the Goddess. No matter. Prejudice occurs inside and outside the ranks of every past and present religion.

Although the early Christians attempted to practice what their Master had taught, the authentic writings about these practices were either lost or hidden, as part of the necessary Resistance movement to the 'churchianity' sweeping through the middle east into Europe through the first four centuries after Christ 's death. Then, in 1945, thirteen leather-bound codices were found in Nag Hammadi, Egypt (the Gnostic Gospels). This was as significant a 'find' as the Dead Sea Scrolls and contained important lost gospels written by the lesser-known disciples, including Mary Magadalene. Generally speaking, these gospels, which have been more accurately translated, have not been acceptable to the great churches.

GALILEO and JEANNE D'ARC

Between the 12th and the 19th Centuries, the Catholic Church and its Popes ordered tribunals to be set up to try, and then to remove, heretical thinkers, either with the death penalty, or by imprisonment.

The two most famous Resistors of this intense and long period of religious persecution were Joan of Arc, and Galileo Galilei – but they Resisted the religion in power for completely different reasons.

Although Joan (Jeanne d'Arc) was tried, convicted and burned by Church authorities for her 'blasphemous declarations' of being guided by God, her motives were initially political. She felt compelled to return power to the French throne from the English pretenders fighting in the 100 Years' War, saying the voice of God told her to do this. Although her efforts and her faith resulted in the French victory, her courageous insistence on heavenly intervention in this political matter is what heralded her own death.

The motivation for Galileo was to free science from religious intervention, and his courage and insistence on the truth of his calculations also led him to his imprisonment. Yet his stubborn Resistance to authoritarian threats, and his keen observation, have made him a household name.

OPIUM

The adage, *'Religion is the opium of the people'* (Karl Marx) may no longer apply. This phrase refers to the dulling of awareness and illusory nature of the drug. However, all around us, are 'masses' of people who are prepared to fight to the death for their beliefs, or at least the right to practice their religion. Theirs is not a 'dulled' path – but their awareness of the experience of inner truth might be. For many, their fanaticism has brought contraction (rather than expansion, growth or development), and a Resistance to seeing any other point of view.

However, there are notable examples in recent decades, of religious people being prepared to fight for the civil rights of others, notably Rev Martin Luther King (in America) and Desmond Tutu in South Africa,

Happily for many, their inner religion has given them an awakening rather than an opiate, where deep contemplation and heart-centred focus has brought mental and spiritual expansion.

It is said that *'when the student is ready, the teacher appears.'* However, the teacher may not be what one unconsciously expects him or her to look like.

Cue Resistance!

PHILOSOPHY, METAPHYSICS and DESCARTES

It appears that the subject of Metaphysics has enjoyed several stages of popularity. The word comes from 1st Century BC Greek, meaning *"following physics."* It may be found in a treatise on Physics, by Andronicus, who had been studying the works of Aristotle.

For the late Greeks and early Romans, it was a general subject, covering all forms of reality, and included philosophical questions on the nature of ultimate reality. These questions were put, and then argued using rationalisation, until considered proven. The answers were founded on *'a priori knowledge, knowledge derived from reason alone, and held to be true of all things'* (Wikipedia) Galileo challenged this way of exploration, in that he was possibly the first scientist to alter his perception of reality, based on *"a posteriori knowledge, which is gained by reference to the facts of experience."* and observation, using logic.

In medieval times, metaphysics was known as the *"trans-physical science"* on the assumption that, by means of it, the scholar philosophically could make the transition from the physical world to a world beyond sense perception. The 13th-century Scholastic philosopher and theologian, St. Thomas Aquinas, declared that *"the cognition of God, through a causal study of finite sensible beings, was the aim of metaphysics."*

However since then, the philosophical study of metaphysics has fundamentally involved a decision as to whether to adhere to the belief that the universe is essentially *monistic* (that everything can be boiled down to one substance) or *dualistic* (ditto, into two substances) or else consisting of an infinite number of substances, called *monads*. There are also the *'empiricists'* who base their philosophy only on things that may be experienced.

The most famous dualist was the Frenchman Rene Descartes, who maintained *'that body and mind are radically different entities and that they are the only fundamental substances in the universe.'* (Encarta) Dualism, however, does not show how these basic entities are connected, thus assuming that they are not.

Still another school of philosophy has maintained that, *'although an ultimate reality does exist, it is altogether inaccessible to human knowledge, which is necessarily subjective because it is confined to states of mind. Knowledge is therefore not a representation of external reality, but merely a reflection of human perceptions.'* This view is known as *'scepticism'* or agnosticism with respect to the soul and the reality of God.

EARTH WISDOM, and BASES for the NEW AGE

All around the world, and in every culture, there have always been the keepers of the earth-lore. These were, and are, those whose feeling for and respect of the land, has allowed them to read the subtlest clues concerning the needs of their land, and its people. In Southern Africa, the little Bushmen who were the 'first people', knew their land and how to survive its' harsh realities. They were 'tuned in' through the seasons as they unfolded over time. They developed complex rituals and healing procedures that were the natural outcome of living in their land and climate

In the Pacific, the Kahunas of Hawai'i and their counterparts in the other Pacific islands, and the Maori of New Zealand all had healing abilities and knowledge of 'occult' (hidden) laws that we in the West still know very little about – but an increasing number are once again practicing and teaching them. However, many of their most secret teachings, in all their subtlety, may go to the grave with the last of these extra-ordinary people.

In the Americas, the Native American 'Indian' lore has, despite the efforts of their colonisers, become a central part of the unwritten 'New Age' 'bible' – respect for the land and ecology, the use of drumming in healing, and the medicine wheel of ritualised acknowledgement of and integration of the 5 elements and 7 directions (above, below, left, right, behind, before and within).

In Australia the telepathy, navigation skills and story-telling memory of the Aboriginal people is still legendary. Again, there are very few Aboriginal people left who are still able to use these skills, This is because there have been such profound changes over these last 250 years – especially for a people that had never experienced colonisation before in their 40,000 year history. No wonder so many choose alcohol to help them deal with the core-level of invasion by our Western 'civilisation', whose mentality is completely alien to them.

Meanwhile in Europe, the Earth Wisdom people, the most well-known being the Celts, paid enthusiastic homage to 'the Green Man' or 'Jack-in-the-Green', the expression of the beauty of the forest and the bountiful provision of food and shelter. The Druids are still allowed by presiding authorities, to practice the honouring of the midsummer sun rising once a year at Stonehenge, There will be a few among them that know fuller versions of the more well-known rituals, and their deeper meaning.

Eastern Schools

In Japan and China, there have been exponents of the current religions mostly among Buddhists, who developed various martial arts, as a means of using the esoteric knowledge they had, and demonstrating its' power.

India has been the birth place of many well-known and deeply-loved Masters, both male and female. The tradition of the saddhus, sanyasins or renunciates, is well known and respected in India, and many of them know and live by metaphysical laws, in the atmosphere of acceptance that surrounds them in their culture. It has been said by Indian sages concerning this time in our history, that we now live in the (tail-end of the) Kali Yuga or time of darkness and greatest Resistance to enlightenment.

The Hindu religion has given us immense understanding of our Universe, in terms of its explanation of Duality. Duality is the name given to the quality of being two-fold that exists in all the opposites that we see in the world. That is: female and male, right and wrong, black and white, light and darkness. It is seen in Hinduism as indicating the level of consciousness of most of humanity, where most people are unable to understand beyond their view of 'good and bad.' Hinduism and modern philosophies present a further sought-after state of awareness – that of knowing the One-ness of all things, which is a state of non-ordinary awareness that lies beyond Duality.

This understanding is borne out by the overview in physics that all things are made of the same 'stuff' in different states of being (waves or particles).

Egyptian Temples

Returning to the Middle East, the Egyptians of the third and fourth centuries BC trained many initiates in their temples. Even the Pharaohs, whether male or female, were trained spiritual initiates in the earlier dynasties. The scribes used symbols to portray metaphysical laws, within the hieroglyph system of transmitting information. It is still being discovered how knowledgeable they were, for instance in the mathematical sizing, angulations, and locations of the pyramids and the sphinx, and its hidden treasures, in relation to star systems in the skies of their times. These stone structures are proving to be the most enduring of all buildings in history.

METAPHYSICAL PRINCIPLES

From many of these sources, a fusion has occurred - a fusion of different Metaphysical principles and Indigenous traditions, as understood and practised by many round the world today. Some of the principles come from many sources, as universal truths, and some have come from a single culture, such as that of the Native Americans.

Now, all these principles appear to have been 'thrown in the melting pot' of today's homogenised culture. But the teachers who resonate with aspects of these principles, draw out and individualise those aspects, and use them to help their students on the journey of gaining a deeper understanding of life.

But the Principles remain the same. Here is an 'alphabet' of these principles, in no particular order. They are likely to resonate with most people, even if the words used are not entirely familiar.

A) The One-ness of all things
Although this principle is at the heart of all religions too, it seems they are all too busy fighting to be the ones who are 'right', to be able to put this principle into practice. Yet we all know the truth of this statement. Scientists are finding ways of explaining this, beginning with the discovery of the atom, and ending so far with a

kind of 'primordial subatomic glue', and 'string' to hold it all together – all of which crosses multi-dimensional universes. Until the last 30 years, Jean-Paul Sartre's Existentialism may have been the closest philosophy we have had, for explaining the inter-connectedness of all things.

So, the flapping of a butterfly's wings in Russia really does affect me here. Apparently even a humble fly stops a train momentarily when it hits the windscreen, speaking at microscopic levels of course.

The Tao Te Ching states: 'The Tao gave birth to One, the One gave birth to Yin and Yang, and the Yin and Yang gave birth to all things.'.

The words below are purported to have been spoken by Chief Seattle, and have become a basis for the ecology movement, and whoever actually did write this, has also put his/her finger on the fundamental principle of the New Age movement at its best.

Man did not weave the web of life; he is merely a strand in it.
Whatever he does to the web, he does to himself."

The parallels between this statement and with the Quantum theories of physical and multi-dimensional inter-connectedness, and the String theory (could this be the web?) cannot escape the observant . It is from this construct that we see how we are connected or related, to all creatures, all walking, crawling, flying, swimming creatures – referred to by the First Nations as 'all our relations.'

B) Thought is Creative

Every thought anyone has affects the planet in some way. Quantum physics shows that the simple act of observing something, along with our beliefs, desires and expectations, alters the probable outcome of what we are observing. This is how we contribute to the Collective Consciousness.

Goal-setting and positive thinking make a difference up to a point, but our underlying unconscious thoughts are strongest.

C) The Creator as Source

God, Goddess, Great Spirit... At the centre of Meta-physics is the observation that there is a Universal Intelligence that is 'in charge.' Jewish scriptures use the Hebrew term Yahweh (the 'Self-Expressing One'), a word without vowels indicating that we cannot fully describe God's vastness. We need to feel our connection with our Creator daily - it is our birthright.

D) Energy cannot be created or destroyed

Since our human body is a coalescence of energies, at death the energy has to be transformed. This may be by fire, into smoke and ash (dust to dust and air or breath of the Earth) or by slow deterioration, reverting back to all the elements. However, what happens to the Soul, that personalised Spirit, when it leaves with the last exhale? Whether it is logical for it to go into another dimension for a different existence, or some other change, the question still remains to be answered. This then takes us into the question of 'what, if anything, was there before 'me', or where do 'I' go after death – what happens to the energy that is currently 'me'?

The explanation of Reincarnation seems the most logical, or at least an 'after-life.' Without continuous transformation, it would appear that this life is wasted and without purpose, and that we can only learn a small part of what needs to be learned.

E) You reap what you sow / What goes around comes around / The Law of Karma

We are here to learn, and we do so through experience or through being healed or by being in service. Or by any combination of these in a lifetime. The phrase 'what goes around comes around' is the current version! We are also here to learn to be happy and in a state of gratitude in the middle of it all.

F) Energy can get blocked in our bodies

It is seen that, not only the fluids of life flow in our bodies, but the energy of life does so too – brought in with every breath. This is called the Prana, Chi, Life Force, Elan Vitale, and is seen by many as our gift from God. This life force, invisible but essential, (and of the Essence), moves everywhere, and is also more concentrated at 7 places in the body, called the major Chakras, or wheels of energy. Some people can 'see' or 'feel' the Chakras, and imbalances or deficiencies in their motion.

Each of the 7 Chakras relates to an aspect of evolutionary man, from simple and basic survival (the lowest Chakra, located around the tail or coccyx) to personal sexuality and power (Chakras 2 and 3) to the heart and the ability to love (4th), the throat (5th) the Ajna or Third Eye of inner vision, to the Crown Chakra (7th) that allows in spiritual frequencies.

G) What you Resist persists

Aha, you may say! Back to the subject at hand. Back to the purpose of the book. What this means is that, any fear that is not healed, continues to affect us. As a survival-based animal, human beings have an inbuilt tendency to avoid pain. This is completely understandable.

If we Resist the call from our deepest self to heal our fears, by facing them, it will become a further Resisted fear. And so, it will remain in our cellular memory – it will persist – until we choose, or build up the courage, to face it. Usually that courage comes from necessity – a wake-up call from a near-death experience, the death of a loved one or close relationship ending, or a life-threatening illness.

To make matters worse, the accumulation of negative or sticky energy from that fear, may well lead to any of the events above, presumably by causing a sort of 'eddying' in the energy flow, and local stagnation, leading to sickness or rejection. It seems cruel in a way, and yet that's how it appears to be. The very act of Resisting a truth about ourselves will actually draw to us an increasing amount of energy to make us "wake up" – as if it is magnetised by our 'sticky' blinkers. But the intention is not to simply expose our blind spots, but to take us beyond them and into enlightenment, through healing them.

However help is at hand – we don't have to go through all these painful moments alone – there are always 'angels' who pop up to help us, if we care to look and listen to the clues.

Thus, the opposite of Resistance, that is "Allowing" or Acceptance, is the principle in motion. There is no point in Resisting the Resistance – by pretending it's not there, or fighting it, or even by forcing oneself to look at it prematurely

H) To everything there is a season

Timing is all. Time heals all, ultimately. And trying to force a healing too soon – usually out of fear of the consequences – is unlikely to work very well. Somehow, at the right moment, when there seems to be a 'flow' of events and support, the healing will be experienced deeply, and so it will affect deeply too. Do not judge apparent procrastination – there is always a reason and a season.

I) Coincidences / Synchronicity

Clearly conveyed to us in the book 'The Celestine Prophecy' (Redfield), we notice that, as we start to expand our consciousness, we see increasing evidence of Synchronicity, which appears, initially, as 'Coincidences.' We start to see the flow of life, as we dance in and out of each others' lives.

J) Consequences

Further to point (E), everything we do, or every action we take has an equal and opposite reaction. There are always consequences and there are advantages and disadvantages to absolutely everything. As it becomes clearer how even our small choices are likely to have long-term consequences, so we need to make a comprehensive decision to become more conscious. By making the ultimate vision more important, the smaller consequences can be more easily dealt with.

K) What you focus on, expands

This is the principle whereby energy flows to where the attention is. So when goal-setting, if you want something a lot, putting a large amount of attention on that desire will probably bring it to you. But it is also said 'be careful what you wish for, you might just get it' (and all of its consequences!). In addition, if you focus on the current lack of something in your life, namely money, love, work etc, that is what will most likely increase. Focusing on what you enjoy will increase its manifestation.

L) Intention alters everything

What is your greatest Intention in life? We can have the overall intention to heal our difficult areas', to look into the eyes of the 'paper tiger' that we fear, to admit to our Resistances in life. In this, we approach Enlightenment and Ascension and the gift of resting in the company of Masters, Sages, & Higher Beings. Now is the time to affirm your commitment to loving yourself. Reach out to know and be known, beyond your highest vision.

M) Body and Mind are One

This principle is almost more important than all the others, simply because the belief in the separation of the two, has caused more disturbance in recent human evolution than any other belief. (since poor Descartes, the product of his time, made this emphasis in his understanding of our nature). Body and mind are totally inter-pervasive. Ripples of one flow through the other, and each one reflects the other. The body is the mind. The mind is the body. If you 'upgrade' your values, it will continue to reflect in your health and body-awareness.

N) The truth of Cellular memory

In the study of Psycho-Neuro-Immunology, it is now accepted that memory and its associated emotion, functions through chemical changes in cells all over the body, not just the brain. If an incident such as a trauma occurs, it gets attached to the cells in the region associated with that event. If we could 'read' each cell, we would be able to tell details of each others' stories, rich and complex as they are.

O) 'Attitude of Gratitude' (an expression of Reverend Ike)

This principle used to be called 'counting your blessings' - of what is positive and good in your life. There is ALWAYS something or someone good in our lives. The experience of gratitude also acts as a magnet, drawing further beautiful experiences to us. Walking down the street, seeing, hearing, smelling beauty is a real blessing. It is a gift we are fortunate to be born with and need to develop and use, and encourage .

P) Forgiveness

To allow forgiveness of past hurts and trauma is possibly the most profound gift we can give ourselves. In doing so, we free our lives, our selves, our bodies, and those of the perpetrators of abuse we experienced, either personally or in the ancestral line back in time (remember, time is not always linear, even though it appears that way) and forwards in time for all our descendants for 7 generations. The learned state is Discernment, so we don't repeat mistakes that set us up for harm. 'Forgive us our trespasses, as we forgive those who trespass against us...'

Q) Frequencies, Vibration and Resonance

All things are vibrations of energy. Our bodies seem dense, but actually consist of more space than matter, lying between the electrons and nuclei of all atoms. In fact we may be 95%+ Void (which is Creative Potential) in our cellular molecules The same is true for everything that surrounds us, and includes all feelings, thoughts, dimensions and spirit. Whatever we resonate with in terms of frequency, we will attract or be attracted to, invisibly, 'across a crowded room', street or continent. Interestingly, vibration is created by opposites alternating.

R) The 100th monkey principle.

The story goes, as written by Lyall Watson, then by Ken Keyes, that the habits of the monkeys on one small island 'spread' to monkeys in adjacent but un-reachable islands. After a certain number of monkeys learned this trick of dunking their sweet potatoes in the sea to salt them, others 'copied' this new technique for simian gastronomy, without actually being taught directly.

In other words, the monkeys would be demonstrating the 'Morphic Resonance' as described by Rupert Sheldrake (first in 'Hypothesis of Formative Causation') demonstrating how we are all connected. Although this may not be exactly correct, in terms of research, the 'urban legend' of the '100th monkey effect' is as powerful as the previously mentioned speech of Chief Seattle's. Whether it is disproved or not, it is a very graphic way of describing the 'Critical Mass' principal. However, looking around us, we notice that increasing numbers of people appear to understand the aforementioned principles far more quickly than used to be the case. This could be the action of this particular principle in operation. The more people there are who seek consciousness, the more people will 'get it', and more quickly too.

S) 100% Self-Responsibility

When we take 100% responsibility (not 50-50) for how our world is happening around and within us, it becomes impossible to blame anyone or anything else. 'The buck always stops here.' This is possibly the hardest of the principles to take on board. It can be intensely uncomfortable, yet it can also bring relief. 'If I have made it this bad, I can also 'un-make' it', I am not a powerless victim.

To help in understanding this principle, imagine you are in a swimming pool. Alone there, you make ripples that are visible. But in the company of others, the ripples all interfere with each other & it becomes hard to see who is impacting who. However, with perspective, what made you jump in that pool at that particular time with those particular people? That is where the choice lies. This principle was indicated by Jesus when he directed us to 'love your neighbour as yourself', and when followed-through, is earth-shaking in the magnitude of its repercussions.

T) What you can't communicate, runs you

Imagine a person in love. But he or she is unable to tell the object of his affection. Does this make it easier for him to be around this person? Does it make for a focused day at work? No. He is driven by his unspoken passion. Now imagine a person who has been told by a family member to keep a secret, large or small. Every day a noticeable portion of his thoughts will be taken up with the inner conversation about this.

Now imagine a person who has been hurt so deeply by an event early in his pre-verbal years. There cannot be an inner conversation about that for obvious reasons. But it will have an effect on his whole view of life, his expectations of people, of life itself. This will be like looking through 'not-rose-tinted-glasses' and will affect everything he looks at in his life.

But when he starts to find these lost parts of the jigsaw of himself, sooner or later he will experience an 'Aha' moment of realisation, that the world is not necessarily the way he has seen it all his life after all. Until that point, he will be 'run' by that view of life, the universe and everything.

U) My results are my teacher

We are the architects of our own worlds and what we see 'out there' is the best way of discovering what we unconsciously believe and add energy to. Looking around us at our worlds and our experiences, we begin to see the possibility hat they have been projected and manifested from our unconscious, in order to help us heal vital aspects of our psyche.

V) Energy flows along the POLR – the Path of Least Resistance

This is a physical law, as well as a metaphysical one. As the latter, we see that energy, which is being used to create every aspect of every day, must flow where it can do so easily. If we have a 'block' to receiving money, for example, it will be very hard to win the lottery – or to keep the money without spending it all as soon as possible, if we do win somehow.

W) 'You have $100 of energy a day to spend as you like'

Caroline Myss authored this metaphor of how we divide the energy we receive daily. It is as if we are given $100 a day by the Creator to spend as we wish. That sounds great until we see that we spend the greater part of it on regret, guilt, fear of the future, past hurts or unreasonable demands on ourselves and others. These negative thoughts act as a drain on our inner resources, and end up limiting what is being given to us afresh each day.

X) 'Love Brings Up Anything Unlike Itself – for Healing and Release'

This principle comes from the Course in Miracles. In the presence of love, whatever is not of the nature of love within us, will surface. In loving relationships, anger, jealousy, hatred, fear, sadness, guilt, will sooner or later show up. When that happens, thank the person for loving you enough to help surface what's unhealed – they are being your soul-mate, your greatest teacher.

Y) From the summarised HUNA principles: (ancient Hawai'ian teachings expounded by Serge King)

1) IKE	The world is what you are aware of	Be Aware
2) KALA	There are no limits to forgiveness	Be Free
3) MAKIA	Energy flows where attention goes	Be Focused
4) MANAWA	Now is the moment and core of power	Be Here Now
5) ALOHA	To love is to be happy with	Be Happy
6) MANA	All power and energy comes from within	Be Confident
7) PONO	Balance, with Reconciliation	Be Positive

The process of Ho'opono'pono is basically that of forgiveness, and Reconciliation, especially in an ancestral and family context.

Z) "Man, Know Thyself"

The Delphic Oracle summarises it all.

CHOICE

Finally, it is up to the inner thirst of the 'seeker' to deal with his or her inner Resistance usually by one fundamental choice, one decision, made at the deepest level. It all begins with a question to oneself: *Am I happy with my life as it is?* If the answer is 'no, the choice becomes clear: to choose to become conscious, whatever it takes. One can keep coming back to that basic choice at any time, whenever the faith in the process becomes shaky or 'scary.' The journey then lasts a lifetime – maybe longer !! But of course you will never be the same again. Sometimes this feels good, bringing it's own rewards of inner peace. Sometimes it feels awful. But there's no going back – you can't un-know something that you know. But then what is the alternative? Life as it was, no longer satisfies – not really, not for long.

Dharma the Cat & Co.
courtesy of
www.DharmaTheCatCartoons.com
Philosophy with Fur

The MULE's EYE VIEW

If the Mule is to be believed, all progress is digress and egress, and necessitated by the frequent use of carrots. But in one particular area, he would show his natural wisdom: he would never put Des Cartes before de horse!'

Joking aside, a Portuguese-Brazilian myth tells the story of a cursed headless female Mule that gallops around the region, which houses a sinning priest and his lover, and is dangerous to behold. It embodies a wild and headless passion that leads 'men of God' astray from celibacy, through the power of the feminine

EVIL, TEMPTATION and MORALITY

To finish on an important religious issue, it has been said (by Joseph Fulda) that man is in charge of his character, and God is in charge of the magnitude of his 'temptation', knowing in His omniscient way, what that person can handle and what is needed for his evolution. In this manner, God has sovereignty over what is placed before us to learn from. However, we employ our Free Will as we make choices about what to do with this 'temptation.' We can then succumb to it, or Resist it. God then supplies 'Plan A' or 'Plan B' for the next stage of development.

But I say unto you, That ye Resist not evil, but whosoever shall smite thee
on thy right cheek, turn to him the other also. (Matt 5:39)

"Has any country forgiven anyone recently? Or are we continuing to be a society of endless blame and punishment? People seem to assume that the moment you brand someone else as evil (terrorists, Nazis, mass murderers, paedophiles, etc.), you have every right to seek revenge against them. The War on Terror is based on this notion. *"Resist not evil," if carried out in real life, would lead to a society of forgiveness."*   Deepak Chopra – 2005

I believe we have quite a way to go before we are ready for this. A simple understanding of this radical guidance is that we need to learn to 'Resist the sin, but love the sinner.'

Chapter 5 – Political Resistance

Of: Resistance fighters and movements;
Dreadlocks and berets and human rights
Civil Disobedience & Passive Resistance

'Vive la Résistance!'
"Resistance occurs in a dis-integrated society .Liberty has never come from the government. Liberty has always come from the subjects of it. The history of liberty is a history of Resistance. The history of liberty is a history of limitations of governmental power, not the increase of it." Nadia Boulanger
"The British Empire, the greatest Empire of modern times, began its collapse in India with the so-called Passive Resistance Movement led by Gandhi, which was so passive that it could hardly be said to "resist" at all! And future historians will probably say that one of the major forces in twentieth century America has been the "Non-Violent Movement for Social Change" inaugurated by the Rev.Martin Luther King' #38 in the Swedenborg Digital Library
War is a symptom Prem Rawat
In politics, what we resist, desists, eventually CCJ
'If you want to taste a pear, you must change the pear by eating it' Mao
'Resistance to violence is never useless… (but) to wage war, one must believe in an enemy. If we refuse to be enemies, how can they fight us?' Starhawk

As long as colonisation, oppressive regimes or attitudes occur within a nation, there will be large groups of people that Resist any restriction of personal freedom, and the loss of connection with the land of their ancestors. These are the Resistance movements, known throughout history, but acknowledged as a grass-roots, counter-reaction since the advent of widespread and rapid reporting – that is, since the mid 1900's.

Examples of such regimes that have stirred up Resistance Movements, are the armed Maquisards of the French Resistance movement in World War II who opposed not only the Nazi invasion of France, but also the Nazi desire for world dominion. This example of Resistance fighters is perhaps the most 'famous' - so much so that they have become part of folk-lore. South Africa prior to May 1994, where the fight against white-dominated Apartheid, took 42 years to take effect, is another recent example that has taken on archetypal proportions.

But any colonised nation, for example: Singapore - colonised by England, Japan and then Malaysia after WWII, produced its own Resistance fighters. Or there may be Resistance within a system where there is an apparent equality in terms of numbers – such as RAWA (the Revolutionary Association of Women of Afghanistan) is an ongoing example.

We are currently witnessing this situation in many countries: RAWA in Afghanistan, the Palestinian situation, Mugabe in Zimbabwe (whatever we think of his means and results, Resistance to colonisation was his initial motivation), Fidel Castro in Cuba (although while writing, he is bowing out of politics and handing over to his brother); and Northern Ireland. In Myanmar (Burma) the peaceful advocate and figure head for majority rule is Aung San Suu Kyi. The situation is difficult in Tibet with China, where peace is clearly the preferred option; but for reasons few people understand, the Chinese continue to insist on the suppression of a peaceful race.

THE END JUSTIFYING THE MEANS

Resistance fighters were and are, courageously working to generally maintain whatever is positive and humanitarian in their own culture, and sooner or later have been willing to use any means - fair or foul, to do so. The Resistance is against external control and abuse of power. For the Resistance fighters sometimes, the 'end justifies the means.' If violence becomes necessary because those in power are not listening, then that is what will be used. Their guerrilla tactics loudly highlight their plight.

Removal of the freedom of self-expression, for people whose ancestral link with that land is ancient, heralds the onset of dissent. Those individuals in Resistance movements over the years often become willing to lose their own lives and even the lives of their families, in order to create a free and just society not only for their own people but also for succeeding generations. Sometimes the desired result may take more than one generation of fighting, which may mean a whole generation grows up not knowing a peaceful way of life. The new generation, born into a time and place where there is endless turmoil, where their families are always looking over their shoulders for sudden attack, constantly in a state of deprivation, of food, of secure shelter and of trust, are stripped of their right of having a happy childhood.

Clearly, wherever there is war, whether within or between nations, there will always be Resistance from one side or the other, although the term Resistance fighter, generally refers to a group of people that would not have taken up arms in the first place. Resistance then becomes the means of expression that unites peoples who may not have connected with each other in times of peace. And because the perceived enemy holds the power rigidly, more inventive means of Resistance have to be found. Unfortunately, to the chagrin of most of the 'oppressed' people, it is usually violence that finally makes the controllers sit up and listen.

It is Ironic, or perhaps not, how often we find that the oppressed peoples become more resourceful, not only in their Resistance activities, but also simply in daily life. And when the fighting is finally over, the celebration and gratitude for freedom is immense, where it may have been taken for granted before the fight for freedom began.

CHANGE

Resistance can be the 'fire' that usually motivates, and results in, positive change. This is a personally held opinion: that there is a long-term purpose in oppressive regimes, and that includes the role of the Resistance forces themselves.

The purpose may be seen that, through change and temporary chaos, the two forces opposing each other together begin to implement the changes necessary to becoming a stronger and more self-sustaining land. In other words, this is a large-scale enactment of 'what doesn't kill you strengthens you', which must be considered with perspective.

Change in itself is Resisted, not only by the controlling power, but also by many of the oppressed. That is because change is about challenging some old aspects of life that have been seen as unchangeable. Which may be why it can take many years to finally throw off the oppressive power that, for many, becomes the 'devil you know', that is, a predicable enemy with whom they can collaborate.

Not all the 'old ways' need to change. Some have worked smoothly for centuries, and the change is destructive, causing disintegration within that society. An example of this is the change in old Yugoslavia, brought about by 'ethnic cleansing' in the previously multi-religious state of relative harmony. The societal trauma accompanying such change, in the creation of the six or seven independent principalities, including Bosnia, Croatia and Serbia, may take several generations to heal. However, Yugoslavia had been divided and unstable for centuries before that, so their civil war may have finally resolved the situation.

So we need to look at what factors invite imposed change from those that invade, or from those who begin a civil war. Sometimes, the war seems to be started purely because of a desire to increase territorial power over a neighbour. It is interesting to look at what even motivates such thought and action. Is it as old as 'sibling rivalry' (Cain and Abel), where the 'grass looks greener' over the other side of the barbed-wire fence? Or is it a simple jealousy concerning available resources, or even the harmony itself of the neighbouring nation, that the aggressor wants to somehow seize?

SEMITIC BATTLES

The clearest example of the Cain-and-Abel phenomenon is the battle between the Arabs and the Jews. Tracing their ancestry back in time to their common beginnings:-

The term Semite means a member of any of various ancient and modern peoples originating in southwestern Asia, including Akkadians (modern Iraqi), Canaanites (Lebanese to Egyptians), Phoenicians (*same geography but more recent*), Hebrews, Arabs, and Ethiopian Semites' (Wikipedia)

In the Biblical sense, their origins can be traced back to Abraham. As Sarah his wife was initially infertile, her Egyptian handmaiden was given to him, and bore him Ishmael. A few years later, Sarah bore Isaac, as Abraham's legitimate heir. She then banished Hagar and Ishmael. Can it really take so many centuries for ancestral jealousy and legalities of birth to burn itself out?

Their descendents not only have their ancestry in common, but also the origins of their language, their shared reverence for several prophets, notably Abraham and also Isaac, and of course their geography. Yet the rivalry between the descendants is greater and more long-lived than any other we know. How long have their heated disputes and violent battles continued? And, again, for how much longer?

Meanwhile, both 'Tribes' have spread far and wide, many members of each still holding aggression towards the other, and some moving into a more global view of their ancestral kin. A noted example of the width of this Diaspora (dispersion of a people) is the little known tribe of Jewish Chiefs that intermarried after their travels had taken them to southern Africa. The genetic traces of this ancestry continues in the tribe of the, now Christian, Lemba. It is even believed that the long sought-after Ark of the Covenant may have been brought south by their people.

RESISTANCE AS PRINCIPLE

Sometimes the motives for conflict are based on principles and empowerment at least for the many individuals who fight, regardless of initial political motives. The American Civil War was begun in a successful attempt to bring equal rights to the black workers, whose labour was making many landowners rich, and keeping ex-slaves poor. Those who Resisted that change, had vested interests in remaining rich and in maintaining an unbalanced power. It is well known that some families were torn apart in their support of one side or the other, and may have even come face to face in battle, consequently having to make an inner decision:- to choose between 'blood or principle' as their highest imperative.

By far the greatest known war of Principle, is that of the Second World War. What would have become of our world if Hitler and other dictators of his time (Mussolini in Italy, Franco in Spain, and Emperor Hirohito of Japan) had not been opposed, or Resisted? It makes some pacifists like myself question what we would have done if we had been born at that time, and been available to fight....?

The most well known drive for Independence is that of the Indian sub-continent that was resolved in 1948 with the retreat of the British colonisers. Mohandas K Gandhi was first employed from India by the Indian residents of South Africa in 1893 to help them establish voting and civil rights. He first employed civil disobedience there. When M K Gandhi took over the Indian National Congress in 1921, he saw how the violence that had preceded his return from South Africa was not working. The British were simply fighting back, matching 'an eye for an eye.' It was he that turned around not only the politics of his own land, but the whole of global history, in his embodiment of non-cooperative peaceful, or Passive Resistance

In the end, his insistence on living his vision of a peaceful solution, with the resultant departure of the colonisers, was so significant that he achieved his objective. He had grasped and worked with a fundamental principle: that is, what you Resist persists. The British could not fight back against a yielding force.

The next person to propagate this principle was Martin Luther King, in his highlighting of the civil rights situation for African Americans. He campaigned for the peaceful means of bringing about improvements in the rights of black citizens. Even his assassination in 1968 did not prevent this necessary change. In fact it further advanced his point, and augmented the process of change.

The WOMEN'S MOVEMENT

This is a huge, international and on-going subject of social conditioning, affecting of course half of humanity – and therefore the whole of humanity. Not only is the subject one of balance of power, but of loyalty, to family, to culture, to ancestral values. The Resistance to change in this context is huge and complex. It is embodied by individuals, by families, by cultures, by nations, and by religions. This Resistance to change knows no gender, no age limit, and no specific form of expression. It is insidious and it is overt. Those individuals who seek, initially for their own personal needs, to challenge or change it, have a long battle ahead, and sometimes with the entrenched beliefs of the women around them, as well as the men. Yet the drive to succeed in increasing numbers in this enterprise is almost as strong as the push for survival. The network of determined intelligent women is widening internationally, and it is only a matter of time before the balance of power is established. From the matriarchal systems of early history, to our current patriarchy, balance is the objective, not matriarchy.

Yet in the Western Feminist movement, when we burnt our bras in the 1960's, we may have sadly sacrificed femininity for feminism. Let us 'hold the vision' of balance in that sense also.

HUMAN RIGHTS, and FASHION

Fashion and hairstyle can also be used, and is sometimes actually essential to avoid detection, as the only means of showing allegiance with the forces of Resistance This has always occurred politically, from uniforms, to a single item of clothing, such as the Basque berets of the Maquis in France.

Where peaceful Resistance is the message, the Rastafarian dreadlocks hair of non-conformity has been the outward demonstration of Resistance to the normal status quo of capitalism. In the case of the Afghani women's movement, fashion (the prescribed burkha, or the fuller chadri) is the outward means of suppression, which represents that which is being fought over – namely freedom of expression for half the population. Today, there are many movements that are fighting for equality in the eyes of the law, and in the eyes of people who are in the majority. From black power, to gay rights, to the rights of women to have equal pay; to the rights of Indigenous peoples in their own countries, in the face of white colonialism. As long as people judge by outward appearances, there will be a need for activists to confront these inequalities

ANIMAL RIGHTS, and the GLORY of the MULE

These same principles of information plus (relative) Passive Resistance are employed by such organisations as Greenpeace, to great effect. Their methods of interposition between the whalers' harpoons and their cetacean quarry are legendary. Although animal rights activists go to extremes to get their point across, they believe their protest is necessary, until laws to protect 'dumb animals' are changed.

In many ways, the context of Resistance movements shows our Mule to have his moments of glory and honour. When machinery and vehicles have broken down, or have been destroyed in battle, the quiet and hardy heroism of the Mule has been legendary. Packed with essential supplies, crossing miles of steep and rocky terrain, many a stranded fighter has been saved by his arrival. This shows that even the most Resistant of protagonists has an important place in the web of life. Sadly however, when Mr Bumble proclaimed 'the law is a ass' in Dickens' Oliver Twist, he was clearly maligning our under-appreciated ungulate. On the other hand, Even the greatest Egyptian Queen, Cleopatra forever glorified asses' milk, by bathing in it for the beauty of her skin !

OUTCOME

The Resistance to the sharing of manipulatively-gained power by the controlling forces, is always and eventually dissolved. But when liberation does come, the de-stabilization that occurs when a Resisting force is removed initially results in chaos. However, as we understand from the theory of Chaos in mathematics (meaning 'predictable unpredictability' within a closed system), all chaos moves naturally to order. Yet, order is innate in chaos. We have to retain that overview, when all around appears unpredictable and frightening.

Chapter 6 - Medicine and Resistance

Of: Modern & Traditional Medicines; Bacterial Resistance
Immunity and Auto-Immunity; Complementary Therapies;

"You do not treat systems, you treat human beings…
What goes on in the mind affects us. Body and mind are so
inter-pervasive of each other I do not know how they ever got separated
in our thinking and our practice."
Irwin Korr, London 1998 - Researcher for Osteopathy

MODERN MEDICINE

Referred to as modern medicine, our Western method of medicine has been with us for perhaps 130 years. We have achieved a huge amount in that time, and yet it is still not fully known how, for instance, aspirin works. Diseases are seen as chemical or mechanical misadventures. How else is it that every disease must have a chemical drug that will fight it, one that will ideally 'target' the appropriate offending cells?. And if that doesn't work, then it is seen that we should remove the "disease/problem" by operation or blast it with radiation.

This opinion is over-simplifying the situation, but the whole medical industry is so glamorised to most of us, that the 'still small voice' of the 'Inner Physician' (Upledger) cannot be heard above the clatter of instruments. What has happened to the self-healing capabilities of the body, that are also very well-documented by the medical world of research? Our bodies have been so over-treated, that we have been indoctrinated to expect push-button healing. Then we are surprised to find that things take time to heal, and discover that the process is emotional as well as physical.

In the modern medical world, Resistant diseases or disabilities are seen as something to be overcome, by force if necessary. This definitely works for some people. The whole development of antibiotics and related immunisations, attest to this philosophy, and to its efficacy. But it doesn't work for all of the people all of the time – nothing does.

In fact, Resistance to those very same life-saving antibiotics, by the ever-adapting expression of Life, is proving to be an increasing problem in the world of infectious diseases. There is no doubt that, by instantly dealing with such diseases, they have been the miracle cure of modern medicine. However, we are now witnessing that time allows adaptation, or mutation, to occur, even among the apparently vanquished bacteria, as they return to us in increasing numbers. Tuberculosis, and syphilis have both returned to our communities and our awareness, for example.

However, for lesser infections, such as those in the respiratory or excretory systems, over-use of antibiotics can also lead to development of the 'superbugs' – bacteria that are Resistant to treatment. These "superbugs", such as the MRSA bacterium can cause even more virulent diseases. This looks like a vicious circle in the making.

Sooner or later it will be necessary to address real causes – not just bacteria 'out to get you' in a hostile world. It is very easy to miss this point. When you are a researcher, keeping your head down, being paid to find the solution, it is so easy to see all bacteria simply as 'the enemy' to be 'finished off for ever.'

So why are these bacteria here, what aspect of our selves invites them in to our immune-deficient bodies?

PNI - PSYCHO-NEURO-(ENDOCRINE)-IMMUNOLOGY and PLACEBO MEDICINE

Nevertheless, it seems that we are entering an era where the relatively new science of *PNI* – Psycho-Neuro-Immunology – is gaining strength. This new science looks into - through research and broad thought - the inter-connectedness of mind and body, as mediated by the nervous, immune and endocrine systems and their effects on and from the psyche (mind). PNI emerged from a large study by Robert Ader, begun in the 1980's, when these inter-connections were observed and measured.

In parallel with such developments, there has been a growing body of evidence showing that there is value (not financially though) in using so-called *Placebo* medicine. It has been shown that about 50% of people in double-blind trials (where the physician is also unaware as to which of the prescribed pills is the placebo) respond to a placebo as fully as do those on the real medication. This gives pause for deep thought – if the body can respond to a 'fake' medication as easily as it does to the 'real thing', where does the Body-mind fit into this picture?

However, one of the reasons for this approach not being used regularly, is the concern over patient permission. Perhaps if people were offered a conscious choice, they might not choose to be worked with in that way. We probably have a long way to go before the greater population is ready to choose this means. However, change is occurring from the grass-roots up, where there is a slow but steady increase in people who wish for more involvement in their own medical treatment, where there is a desire to use the body-mind to self-heal.

I want to make it clear that I applaud the incredible effort put in by dedicated doctors and others in the industry. Their love of humanity and their service is beyond measure. I am speaking about the huge industry of belief systems and control within which these dedicated people have to operate.

IMMUNITY and AUTO-IMMUNITY

Immunity is the name we give to the body's natural defences, our Resistance to disease, illness and injury. The 'guardians' of the body, in greatest numbers in the lymphatic system, the spleen and the thymus gland are the White Blood Cells, or Leukocytes (WBC's) which are produced by stem cells in the bone marrow.

They migrate around the body through the blood – or in the case of the Lymphocytes (one type of which is the T-cell), mostly through the Lymphatic system. Another type of leukocyte is the Monocyte – these are the 'vacuum cleaners' of the body that clean up the debris of dead cells and dead bacteria etc. When these cells insinuate themselves out of the blood stream and into the denser body tissues such as the liver, they become known as Macrophages (Greek: 'big eaters'). They are also responsible for the clean-up of tumour cells, fungus or parasites.

Yet these defenders or Resistors of attack from antigens (foreign bodies) are also involved in the healing process. The macrophages, once they have 'sniffed out' the location of the offending wee beasties, through their receptors of different proteins or peptides, and, amoeba-like, have oozed their way to where they are needed, can begin their essential part in the healing process (Pert, p.160). The 'fighters' carry and create the means of healing.

However, they can also carry the means of tissue breakdown, when too many such cells gather and go into a hyper-response. The possibility of mutating DNA in the cells increases, leading to possible cancerous change (Pert p.168)

Yet when we hear of the 'Boy in the Bubble', who suffered from SCIDS – Severe Combined Immune Deficiency Syndrome for his short 13 years of life, in Texas in the 1970's – we see how it would be to live without immunity, without protection against the microscopic world of opportunistic organisms. We also see how it would be emotionally, to live in a world without physical contact, in a space dominated by fear of that much-needed contact.

According to Leslie Kenton, the body reacts to cooked foods as an invasion, sending WBC's into the intestine with their arrival. However, eating perhaps 80% of raw foods strengthens the body's natural immunity and Resistance to disease, as well as providing essential fibre for the motility of the digestive system. Strangely, when we are under stress, and need good quality nutrition to help us cope, that is when we reach for chocolate. And when the stress reduces, so the quality of the food increases, almost in direct proportion! This lack of self-care also reduces immunity.

Frequent use of X-Rays, in diagnostic capacity, lowers the body's immunity. Their use in radiation therapy for treating cancers, may work by so irritating the immune system that the army of defensive blood cells is woken up and begins to look for and fight the host-defeating cancers.

Finally, laughter truly is the best medicine – it raises our immunity, by stimulating endorphins and encephalin painkillers, and it exercises our breathing and facial muscles. There is the wonderful case of Dr. Norman Cousins has very graphically demonstrated this – he laughed himself to health and fully recovered from cancer in 1965.

Auto-Immunity is the name given to the inability of the body's defences to distinguish its own cells as self, and leads to an immune response to itself, and diseases that exaggerate the normal immune response in unnecessary amounts, causing break-down of certain targeted tissues. However, in small doses, a natural auto-immunity may be needed for the body to summon those necessary defences to deal with young tumours. Strangely enough, parasites themselves are sometimes used medicinally in combating auto-immunity (such as round or hook-worms), to induce a normal immune response that is directed 'outwardly' and away from the self.

A question we can ask is, is there a correlation between an emotional sense of self and an act of summoning up the body's own natural Resistance against ones own tissues? Certainly, as we discover through the PNI studies, and other explanations (Pert, Chopra) that neuro-transmitters and their receptors are trembling on every cell all over our bodies, and are immediately responsive to all changes of emotional state that happen every day, whether we are aware of them or not.

EMBRYONIC DEVELOPMENT

Although the study of embryonic development has shown us the beauty, magic and miracle of human growth in-utero, there is one study that explains the process of differentiation of cells into the multiple organs and tissues of our bodies (by Blechschmidt). For the sake of the subject of this book, one aspect is particularly fascinating: that Resistance is essential to growth, as part of the Embryological Development Fields.

This particular aspect is termed 'Retension' whereby the expanding cellular mass stretches locally under tension, when it encounters an unyielding mass made up of the previously established cells. This causes some of the cells to develop into more specialised tissues, those of which ultimately create the diversity of our organs. However, when expansion leads to friction in unyielding tissues, it may result in hardening - which is ideal when creating bone and other harder tissues.

CELLULAR MEMORY

It is now established through extensive research that Cellular Memory is undeniable. In other words, it is not only our brains that have memory. Every cell in the body 'remembers' not only past physical trauma to that area, but also past emotional-mental-spiritual trauma that occurred and resulted in stress and tension being stored in a specific location. The cells achieve this miraculous expression of their part in the 'hologram' of the body, by the production of a protein-peptide chain by their DNA in response to that stress.

This neuro-peptide is available for future recognition, by the recurrence of a similar physical or emotional event, and the production of the memorised chemical. This is the basis of the PNI research, and the body universality of neuro-transmitters and receptors, and the exciting new answers it provides.

When a situation that is occurring to the Bodymind, is Resisted, the stress of that Resistance is stored in the body – and there it remains until it is dealt with. This may explain how a condition remains, despite complete cellular replacement and regeneration. In damaged areas: – cells are constantly re-creating themselves, and those that last the longest renew within about 7 years. Then why does the damage seem to remain after that longest possible period?

Are we re-creating the damage ourselves, as an indication of our Resistance to healing? Is this Cellular Memory something that can be passed on with an organ transplant (Pearsall)?

Can this 'Energy Cyst' (as defined by Upledger) be described as a 'point of Resistance' or blockage that is the most frequently attended to by the Complementary Therapies?

RESISTANCE WITHIN THE BODY

It can be said that Resistance is a force that is an essential part of the body's functions. The Resistance arises from pain, or from the fear or threat of pain or disability. Immunity is built against Resistance. Musculature strengthens against Resistance. Another form of the use of this principle is the active constriction of arterial (muscular) walls in order to create a rise in blood pressure. This is essential in order to handle changes in posture and movement, and to push the flow of blood into the smallest vessels. Also, electrical Resistance in the skin and the Sympathetic nervous system allow the body to reflect its emotional state. The potential difference between nervous synapses or gaps, allows messages to jump across – and if the electrical Resistance is increased, there is a delay.

HOLISTIC and COMPLEMENTARY MEDICINES

Although the world of Alternative / Complementary Therapy has not come up with an earth-changing equivalent to Antibiotics – and may never do so – the slower approach often has better long-term results. Not only that, but clients rarely die of iatrogenic ('doctor-induced') diseases in the Complementary sector.

There are numerous sources of herbal antibiotics, many of which have been used by the Drug Industry, in the production of their own medications.

Unfortunately, there is currently a world-wide move to discredit Alternative medicines, paralleled only by the number of herbal remedies that are being patented by the drug industry, in a bid to have control over their use.

The reason given is that it is being done to make the products consistent in quality and dosages etc. which, of course, is not a bad thing. However, the industry is quite capable of doing that without outside control being imposed. And, we may be moved to ask, since when has the drug industry been a source of pristine values?

Here is a simple "How to deal with Resistance in health matters, using different Alternative Medicines" guide. Always remembering that the observer-therapist affects the results, so each practitioner is as different as each therapy offered

1. Allopathic : Zap it with all you've got!
2. Traditional Osteopathy and Chiropractic – Relax it and then sneak up on it;'Cranial' Osteopathy & Cranio-Sacral Therapy. – Be 'with' it, by being aware of it - it will then release itself from the inside out; or, move with it, until it decides it is tired of Resisting release;
3. Naturopathy / Herbal : Support the physiology to strengthen the body's Resistant immunity – then the body's own self-healing will operate;
4. Homeopathy – 'Treat like with like' – allow the Resistance - it will work itself out; Trust the body;
5. Acupuncture – Back up the meridian line to the nearest point of weakness, strengthen that, then work on the blockage (point of Resistance);

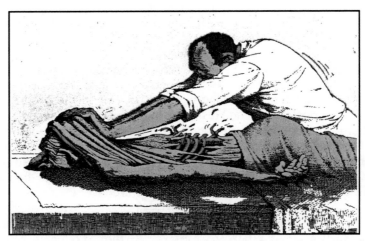

Massage from the 'Resistance School of Massage'(from Serre)

6. Kinesiology – energise the point of Resistance so it gets enough energy to unravel itself, then check up on how you are both doing, using muscle-testing, which is active-Resisted body wisdom;
7. Crystal Healing, and Radionics: identify it, and give it loving support, with these beautiful gifts of Vibrational medicine, from Mother Earth;
8. T'ai Chi – Take the energy of Resistance, work with it, and give it back to the source of aggression – it will then be unable to sustain itself (Taoism);
9. Hypnotherapy – slip underneath the Resistance: Observe, allow, embrace, then utilise it to look at itself, in the Somatised form it has taken;
10. Bio-energetics – Lean into the area of tension (Resistance), allow

the suppressed feelings to surface and release, relax and integrate;

11.   Alexander Technique and Feldenkrais – think beyond it;

There are many other wonderful and inventive therapies, but these are the oldest, most well known and, in a sense, foundational alternatives known. Practitioners themselves are aware of the factor of inter-personal 'chemistry' or vibration / resonance, as well as that person's expectations of improvement, in a patient's response to the treatment and to the therapist.

Osteopathy and Cranio-Sacral Therapy

I will now write a little more about Osteopathy and Cranio-sacral Therapy, because this is my own area of expertise and experience, and also because the general philosophy is common to other therapies in the field. This saves space, and allows for the intelligence of the reader.

<u>Osteopathy</u> This system of Complementary therapy was developed by an American doctor called Andrew Taylor Still in the 1870's. His own personal tragedy, of powerlessly witnessing the deaths of 3 of his children to meningitis, led him to search beyond the then current, limitations of medicine. His attitude was that nature always provides the remedy to all humanity's ills.

He looked to the human body for the source of answers, finding them especially in the freeing up of local and general blood-flow. He used a mixture of localised massage and joint mobilisations, as well as gentler techniques to induce stimulation of the body fluids. He reckoned that health followed the reinstating of motion to the area, allowing cellular nutrition.

Some Osteopaths use the more traditional techniques described above whilst others have particularly taken to the process developed, in the States by the Osteopath, Dr William G. Sutherland in the early 1900's.

These techniques are particularly applied to the skull, or cranium and the term 'Cranial' Osteopathy seems to have stuck. But those who have experienced it know that this system of healing refers to the gentle approach, rather than the actual location of its application. In this context, this gentle 'cranial' approach is able to induce deeper relaxation of stressed tissues than more (structurally-) superficial massage and other techniques.

Since then, other practitioners who have witnessed the unexpectedly profound effectiveness of this approach have created trainings, for non-osteopaths, in *Cranio-Sacral Therapy*. This kind of treatment produces similar results to Osteopathy and has an increasing following. CST Practitioners are happy to recognise and give due credit to the osteopathic origins of the therapy they practise.

As for working *with* Resistance in tissues, some practitioners prefer to work only with the point of health, to strengthen what is already stronger, and to then mobilise the body's own self-healing abilities. My personal opinion is that the focus of attention is less important than the deepest Intention (as opposed to trying to 'fix' someone) of the practitioner – that is where the interface lies with the greatest healing.

The best analogy I can give is that of the Fable of the 'Cold Wind and the Sun.' (As this is a hemispherically-correct book, the reference to the North wind, as spoken in the original fable, would mean a *cold* wind only to those in the Northern Hemisphere!). The story goes that these two elements were arguing about who could most easily remove a man's overcoat. The cold wind blew harder and harder, to try to force it off the man's back. But it was the sun's warmth that encouraged the man to want to remove his coat. In equal measure, the 'cranial' approach is so gentle as to encourage, rather than more forcefully causing the body to let go of the tensions and traumas that we carry in our bodies.

METAPHYSICS

The most thorough and well known study of the connection between mind and body and its results as 'causative' factors, can be found in books by Louise Hay. This modern study of the Body-mind and its interpretive understanding of the causes of dis-ease, is better considered through Chapters 12 and 13.

Chapter 7 – Sports and Resistance

Of: Weight-training and Martial Arts
Working with Antagonists

What you Resist may make you stronger
Without Resistance you cannot climb a mountain
Another word for "Resistance Training" is "Life"
'Aeroplanes require air-Resistance to fly' – Anthony Robbins

RESISTANCE TRAINING

Resistance is known in the field of sports to be a valuable tool in stretching and strengthening one's body. It is most directly used in the field of Weight-training, or Resistance Training, where the body-builder or the athlete chooses whether to go for repetition of a movement, in order to achieve endurance, or for increased weights, to achieve extra strength. The Resistance used, in the form of the amount of weight, or the strength of the 'Resistive (long rubber) Band' worked with, is calculated for achieving the desired results. If a certain muscle-group is strengthened, the 'antagonists' of that group, or those muscles that oppose its action, will be relatively weaker. Our own body can be used to generate Resistance, as in Pilates, isometrics, or by using our own body weight as in press-ups.

An excellent source of Resistance is water. Swimming is a form of repetitive exercise, while finding the least Resistance for an aerodynamic smoothness of travel, and exercising the body and heart muscles thoroughly. The most useful aspect of swimming for older or overweight people is that the body is relatively weightless in this medium, so that exercise feels good, and all the joints can be exercised without putting the extra strain on them which results from merely moving one's own weight on land.

Another clear example of the use of Resistance in sport is Archery. The more the bow is tightened by stretching the cord, the harder it is to do so, and the further the arrows will fly. Letting go of the arrow at that last moment feels wonderful, watching the instant effect of direct physical effort against Resistance. Especially when you hit the target!

Anyone who has ever walked over fine sand will know how much harder it is to do so than on firm land, unless you're a water-snail! The natural Resistance of pavement provides a firm surface to push against, while the sand yields a little under foot. Good for the calves!

The INNER GAME

Tim Galwey has written several wonderful books, all related to what he calls the 'Inner Game' – of Tennis, Golf, Music, and of Work. He is also a sporting instructor in the States, and looks at inner motivation, at how we cause ourselves to stumble in our game or music playing, especially at the 'expert' end of the spectrum. This is where the inner voice can set up forms of Resistance, especially to the actual act of achievement. This very self-sabotaging voice usually gets stronger the closer we get to our desired results. He has devised ways for people to deal with that inner negative voice, so that they can go on to achieve whatever they set out to do.

THE MULE in SPORT

Mule racing & Mule polo are taking off in the USA, especially now they are cloning the (female) winners.

The MARTIAL ARTS and T'AI CHI

T'ai Chi means flowing as a river. Thinking of the qualities of the river, we see that it flows along the path of least Resistance. It doesn't struggle or Resist its journey. It doesn't demand to flow uphill or away from the sea. It moves and dances, tumbles and rages, always and always surrendering to its destination, drawn magnetically to its final rest.

The principle of this most powerful of Martial Arts is to work with a person's Resistance This is why it is the most powerful of these arts. In a contest of 2 masters at the same level of mastery, one of T'ai Chi and the other of say Karate, the master of T'ai Chi will usually win, using the more aggressive energy of the other form, to send the attack back to its source. This balanced use of Resistance is also employed in Ju Jitsu and Judo, where its discipline demonstrates that it is self-defeating to work against Resistance.

In the field of Aikido, a way to practice how to be an immovable object in the face of difficulty, is to imagine and affirm that one's arm (for example) is as strong and as rigid as iron, right through to the finger-tips. When one tries to move someone in that state of certainty, it becomes impossible to do so.

T'AI CHI PRINCIPLES OPERATING IN LIFE

When someone comes with destructive energy, the most powerful response is to allow that force without Resisting it. If one lets the assailant continue on his own trajectory to its natural conclusion, the energy itself will run out as the person falls over or is stopped abruptly against a tree or a wall. Or else one can work with it, and turn it around so that the force of that destructive energy is skilfully turned against its source, and the perpetrator meets their own force head-on, and it either hurts them in its own resolution, or gets burnt out in some other way. But there is also yet another way this principle can be used.

Here is an excellent example of Mastery in this form of thinking – in perhaps an unusual context. Sondra Ray describes a time when she was leading a personal growth workshop, of a few hundred people, where a man suddenly got up and started walking purposefully towards her in an aggressive, antagonistic manner. She describes everything slowing down, as it does around a potentially life-threatening situation.

But during that process, this principle of T'ai Chi came into her mind – to yield and not to fight a stronger force. Instead of Resisting his aggressive energy, she 'drew in' the energy she saw coming at her, and pulled it into her heart, and completely 'let him in.'

As he arrived at the level of her feet, he suddenly physically collapsed on the ground, and he fell into the emotional space that lay beneath his aggression, crying at her feet and asking for forgiveness, which of course she gave.

In fact she had forgiven him before he arrived, which was probably the thing that allowed him to drop beneath that rage. Ultimately this is the deeper desired result of training in the Martial Arts.

We end on a clear description of jujitsu and Resistance, by Osho, as something to aim for:-

'When somebody attacks you, you have to absorb his energy, not resist, as if he is giving energy to you. Absorb his energy; don't resist. He is not the enemy, he is a friend coming to you; and when he hits you with his hand or his fist, much energy is released from his fist. Soon he will be exhausted. Absorb the energy that is released from his fist. When he is exhausted, just by absorbing his energy you will feel stronger, stronger than ever. But if you resist, you shrink, you become stiff so that you may not be hurt. Then his energy and your energy clash, and in that clash, pain happens.'

Chapter 8 – Humour and Resistance

Of: Entertainment, Bill Hicks, Monty Python,
Swami Beyondananda;

> *"Bathe in De-Light, but don't swim in de-Nile"*   CCJ
> *' These are the 1990's, there's a new motto: 'SHIFT HAPPENS'*
> *'The only way to beat Gravity is with Levity'*
> *"Swami Beyondananda"*
> *"Laughter is the shortest distance between two people."*   Victor Borge
> *'I can Resist anything except temptation.'*   Mae West (Oscar Wilde)

Humour is one of the 'saving Graces' of humanity. When we can laugh at ourselves, our situation, we get back our sense of perspective, we enjoy our lives once more, with all its difficulties and doubts. That delicious twinkle that appears in the eyes of someone who is teasing us is so warm and affectionate, and helps us to wake up and smell the coffee. But for some, being teased brings up intense Resistance, either because teasing was misused by their family, or because they can't or don't want to see themselves as someone else sees them.

There are a myriad of examples of the sweetest humour that exists everywhere, usually in the poorest countries. Here people are laughing and smiling and simply enjoying life, knowing or accepting their place on the world. For them, they are not Resisting their situation – they demonstrate total acceptance, and are probably happier than almost anyone we know who probably 'has it all.' This is about Acceptance, and not, in fact, about what they may or may not have. Such beautiful people in every race and culture are inspiring and encouraging.

There are others whose own culture encourages humour, even about their own Resistance – check out Fawlty Towers for wonderful examples of this. Or Monsieur Hulot in France. The Resistance in question is about having to interact with other people. We laugh because we recognise ourselves, if we're honest.

Laughter is also deeply healing. Dr Norman Cousins healed himself of Cancer in the 1970's, watching Marx Brothers movies, among others. This is how he lightened up, and dropped any Resistance he had to healing.

HISTORY OF HUMOUR

Resistance is well expressed throughout the history of humour. Witness the satire of Geoffrey Chaucer in English literature, where he expressed his dislike of religious hypocrisy in the *Canterbury Tales*. As we know, when there is Resistance towards an authority group, whose words and actions are not appreciated by the majority, sooner or later those around them will find ways of drawing attention to this. They may use humour, often sarcasm, in an attempt to get their message across. It seems that sarcasm is used when people feel powerless, and the humour is delivered with a bite.

In ancient times, however, it was agreed that satires were intended to *'tax weaknesses and to correct vice wherever found'* (Encarta). Satire has been used extensively in past European centuries, to caricature those traits that were seen as expressions of self-importance. It was a way of breaking down the apparent magnitude of someone's social position, and to increase the self-esteem of the 'less fortunate.' Although the satirists were often scathing and even cruel (see the French film, 'Ridicule'), their audience was forced to listen and think about the content of the words.

These days, we may stumble over Shakespearean verse, and yet he wrote for all audiences, so all could be entertained and enlightened at the same time.

Humour has, at its best, been a central part of Resistance movements, that is to say, for the masses of people who question political hyperbole. There are excellent examples of political activists using humour to wake people up. One of the first instances of this that we may remember, from movies in the early 1900's, would be Charles Chaplin, whose 'Great Dictator' film satirised the vanity of Hitler, sometimes without having to utter a word. But his balletic mimicry of the dictator's megalomaniacal posturings made people laugh, and cry. How could such a man be taken seriously as a politician – being named Adenoid Hynkel? It was observations, such as these, during the Second World War that enabled those opposing Nazi control, to find the courage to continue the battle to its inevitable conclusion.

To come closer to the present day, the American comedian Lenny Bruce made an art-form of political satire. He was also very rude and crude, but he was able to question the complacency of the people in power during the 1960's, especially the fanatical fear held by the governing powers concerning Communism, which of course was well-Resisted by many.

TV HUMOUR

From the sublime to the truly ridiculous, there are even some sit-coms that are not only funny, but manage to parody society and laugh at ourselves from a lofty height. For example: '3rd Rock from the Sun' or 'Home Improvement' or 'The Simpsons.'

With the 'Third Rock' story, the 4 'aliens' have apparently landed here and are experiencing Earth for the first time. They have absolutely no Resistance to the experiences that Earth has to offer, and jump in to everything with both feet – then surface to tell the exciting tale. Seeing ourselves through their eyes is hilarious. Once again, we need to stand back and see ourselves from afar, and stop taking ourselves so seriously, and thereby reduce the stress in our lives.

To return to Earth, probably the most earthy, but un-earthed, sit-com would be 'Home Improvement', also from the USA in the 1990's. Our lovable rogue hero, Tim-the-toolman-Taylor, is constantly getting himself into trouble, because of his reluctance (OK, Resistance) to listening to advice. The advice comes from his work colleagues, and his highly intelligent wife, and from the 'mouths of babes and sucklings', or at least his 3 boys. The only person he listens to is the highly educated semi-visible man next door, whose wise words are skilfully distorted by Tim's own simple understanding. He is constantly seeking more power (from his power tools), and creating dangerous accidents. It could be said he needs to increase his Resistors, in order to become more grounded.

'The Simpsons' cartoon characters are shown as the ultimate, lovable dysfunctional family living in an equally dysfunctional township – they Resist normality with flair and have successfully glorified mediocrity – they are a whole Resistance movement in their own right. Namely, Resistance to political correctness, and the homogenised (now 'homer-genised') 'family values' culture, that gave it birth. And yet the undertone is that, despite the obvious dysfunctionality of the family in question, they do all love each other, and therefore ironically, true 'family values' are upheld. Like all slapstick that makes us laugh, the irreverence and extreme misfortune that befall the township also stretch the limits of our empathy. (Joe's bar might get a phone-call from Bart, asking him to find a 'Miss Fortune' there etc – he shouts out 'is there a Miss Fortune here? Everybody else 'gets it' and laughs at him).

Star Trek is not funny. But an occasional vein of wit surfaces in this time-honoured sci-fi series. In 'The Next Generation', the android Data is trying to become human. He has attempted emotions, and now he is trying humour. But he just isn't able to get it. You see, it takes a certain amount of emotional warmth to lampoon life's follies and problems, which are the source of most of human comedy. You could say that Data's Resistors were over-capacitated!

In another of the 'Trekky' series, 'Voyager', one of their crew-members is called "Seven-of-Nine." This is because she had been 'assimilated' by the totally left-brained and very metallic 'Borgs.' (I'm sure the great musician and comedian, Victor Borg would not have been amused) – and then rescued. Apparently the 'Borg' motto is "Resistance is Futile." Well she did (Resist), and lived to tell the tale of having all her circuits rewired. However the over-serious circuit had been left intact. But there was a lovely line in one of the programs, where an acid comment of hers was parried by another crewmember with the retort 'it must have been something you assimilated.' The whole Star Trek series is full of 'explore, get attacked, Resist, resolve, move on.'

Meanwhile, in a sit-com far far away, in terms of sophistication, is the differently-hilarious English space spoof called 'Red Dwarf.' These boys (a hologram, an android, a cat who has evolved over millions of years to look like a human, because of his need to be able to use a can-opener, and a dreadlocks-sporting guy from middle England) are hurtling through space looking for new life. Each character demonstrates different aspects of Resistance. The android is delighted to be useful in any way he can be – he has no Resistance to his fate as the ship's dogs-body or servant. The hologram, however is highly manipulative, and will use any means fair or foul, to avoid (or, of course, Resist) his responsibilities. The human hates being there at all, and his Resistance to any necessary activity can be lowered by a good input of beer and Vindaloo curry, and other forms of entertainment. The cat disdains (Resists) everything, unless it's colour-coordinated.

A wonderful moment of 'the machine-is-alive-and shows-it by-humour' is from the movie 'Short Circuit', when robot Number 5 is grilled by his 'maker', an electrician in the Defence Corps. Eventually he has the idea of telling the robot a joke, and awaits his response. The metallic mechanism gets the joke, and laughs… and here is our sign that he must be alive. The maker has, until that moment,

Resisted acceptance of the robot's aliveness, because this possibility doesn't fit in with his understanding of machinery. However, he is smart enough, when faced with the evidence, to accept the unbelievable.

BILL HICKS

More recently still, the most excellent comedian-philosopher, Bill Hicks took up the torch of Lenny Bruce, with his own brand of penetrating observations about 'the world, the universe, and everything' (to drag into the equation, a quote from 'the Hitchhiker's Guide to the Galaxy'). In a way he was a Resistance Movement all by himself. His piercing rhetoric, cut through any political ploys used to pull the wool over people's eyes. He carefully thought through any evidence given by the powers-that-be and found the flaws in their arguments. He was then able to present this to his audience, with scathing and brilliant delivery. He questioned the Kennedy assassination in detail, looking at the fatal bullet's trajectory. His astute observations have added fuel to the fires of conspiracy theories. The same with the war with Iraq - For example, concerning the first one, which was begun by George Bush's father, Bush Snr: *"How do you know so much detail about the weapons they had?' 'Oh, I looked at the receipt."*

Unfortunately, his delivery makes rich use of our 'Anglo-Saxon' swear words, which makes it hard for some people to hear him. Also, the fact that he is now dead, would decrease his chances of being heard – certainly for live performances. In fact he is becoming more and more of a cult figure, through the internet & DVDs of his work. In my opinion, his death at the age of 33, of lung-cancer was premature, but then some of the best people die at that age. Speaking of which, Bill had a radical and unspoken love of Jesus, if not a sense of being a political and people's oracle himself.

"When Jesus comes back, do you think he'd ever want to see another *#@* cross? It would be like going up to Jackie Onassis with a rifle pendant, saying, 'I'm right with you" ('So, forgive me!')

But the sense he would prefer to leave us with, is his 'fervent prayer' that, *'all the money, all the billions of dollars spent annually on weapons in the world, should be spent on feeding, clothing and housing the poor, not one person excluded.'* He believed that this whole life is 'like an amusement park – so *"hey - don't worry or be afraid, ever, because, This is just a Ride."*

PYTHON

Moving into the area of humour based on the elaboration of religious stories is bound to elicit strong Resistance in those who 'have ears to hear, but cannot hear.' The film by the Monty Python team *"The Life of Brian,"* elicits strong reactions in some quarters. A superficial glance at the story suggests ridicule of Jesus. But further exploration shows that the story takes us to the stable next door, where 'Brian' was born. That is, Brian who is initially mistaken for the Saviour of his time, until his Mum questions the presents brought by the Wise Men.

30 or so years after his birth, Brian and other locals in Palestine, are listening to Jesus on the Mount – who is played very reverently by one of the team, as he gives his beautiful Sermon. The onlookers yell "Speak up, I can't hear you" 'I think he's saying 'blessed are the Greeks.'" Once again, irreverence is used as an affectionate form of Resistance and is aimed at the following:

1 - how wise the men actually were at the birth (they realised their folly and went next door to the right manger)

2 - the level of intelligence of those who were listening – no microphones or recording media, so those far from where Jesus was standing, may well have heard him incorrectly, and anyway might never have truly understood what he was saying;

3 – Political Resistance groups "So tell me, what have the Romans ever done for us? - apart from, hospitals, roads, safe streets & water, plumbing, sewage, plentiful markets, bridges, education…. ?"

4 – People being so determined to have a saviour, that they will not listen - as Brian attempts to get the increasing crowd away from him:- Brian: *"I'm not the Messiah"* - *"He must be the Messiah, because only the true one denies his greatness"* (Brian) *"OK, I am the Messiah;"*Everyone at once: *"you see, he is the Messiah…!"*

5 – the healings – did they all want to be healed, was there any gratitude? Witness the guy who is begging for 'alms for an ex-leper' and hopping around.

6 – Political stupidity – Brian gets a Latin lesson for his anti-Roman graffiti "and don't do it again", after he has painted the grammatically-revised slogan 100 times. (Romans Go Home!)

8 – the final scene, yes the crucifixion scene. Visited by various groups, who look like they're coming to rescue Brian – especially the 'suicide regiment' who defy all logic, and kill themselves in support for his sacrifice.
And why not "Always look on the Bright Side of Life"?

OTHER SOURCES

Other sources of a form of Resistance, through comedy, are:-

a) Ali G – where Resistance meets rebellion, for the recent generation *"So, when is this Global Warming going to happen? I say 'bring it on, bring it on'"* (remembering he lives on England's fair and cool shores)

b) Dame Edna Everage – an older generation of rebellious Resistance, one-on-one style, where she/he can get away with asking some pretty close-to-the-bone questions of the guests, encouraging them to unwittingly reveal how they really think.

c) Then of course there are the impersonators, who provide excellent awareness of political mistakes, by being so direct that they get away with it. On the other hand, the English tradition of political satire was taken to extremes, very effectively, through the glove puppets of Spitting Image in the 1980's, whose caricatures were brilliant, but occasionally went unnecessarily into cruelty.

'SWAMI BEYONDANANDA'

Finally, moving from the ridiculous to the sublime, I would like to introduce you to Swami Beyondananda, the Cosmic Comic who has opened his Clown Chakra. If we were to name where his Resistance lies, it would be to 'closed mindedness.' His form of Resistance is through the New Age, which he teases with the tenderness of someone who has been there and done all of it, who actually rates it highly, but wants to show his affection through teasing. He has a wonderful way of doing so without demeaning. He makes endless puns about New Age terms, so that anyone who hasn't actually 'been there' would mistake his jibes for Resistance to the New Age itself, though indirectly. He plays an Indian with a fake name (Swami 'Beyond Bliss') who talks about every aspect of spiritual self-improvement.

a) Relating a spoof visit to a 'Breatharian restaurant' where the *'atmosphere is terrific'* (after the Ascended Masters golf tournament), he asks his host about the Breatharians, who don't eat or drink but live on Prana.

"What are those people doing walking around with clothes pegs on their noses?" The answer is given : *"Oh they're fasting !"*

b) When asked by a member of the audience about the Earth changes and where to live on the Planet, he replies that as there is an increasing likelihood of earthquakes. So when you are choosing somewhere to live, remember that "the Earth, like any other being, has her Faults! So be kind, and just don't *'dwell on them.'!"*

The 'Swami' demonstrates how it is possible to use humour to get one's point across, without being cruel. His most recent book 'Swami for Precedent' is notable for it's counter-culture of gentler political Resistance too.

The WAY of the JACKASS

The 'pompous fool' has been a favourite of entertainers for millennia. To ridicule the slower-witted but landed gentry, or drongo, has been a way for the less fortunate to feel more powerful, if they were able to laugh at the asinine posturings of those who have had more money and power than sense. And laughter and tomfoolery is perhaps the very best medicine.

Famous Mules: Muffin the puppet Mule; Mr Ed and Francis the Talking Mule - with their cynical and sardonic wit and wisdom, but known only to the one person in the 'know';

May the Farce be with you (from the Swami as above)

Chapter 9 - Music, Art and Resistance

Of: Wordless and Wordy rebellion;
Architecture, Gardening & Feng Shui;

'We are the artist and the art'   Gregg Braden

Drawing by
Richard E.
Jennings
'63

"Art is expression. It requires creativity, imagination, intuition, energy and thought to take the random feelings of uneasiness and dis-satisfaction and compress them into useful expression."   Bogart
"Theatre is the act of Resistance against all odds. Art is a defiance of death"   Bogart

The Arts have always brought pleasure and awakening to all. But they are now being explored in terms of their healing properties - and also in reducing stress and neurone-excitability in business. The new businesses have beautiful works of art, and soothing music – usually classical – playing, to make the working environment conducive to creative team-work and lateral thinking.

ART

Art has always been a transcendent means of communication. It is used to communicate, wordlessly, the artist's opinion of their own world and to share that vision through the archetypal power of images, sound, and constructs. This fact

Guernica
Picasso
1937, after the bombing that brought attention to the
Spanish Civil War

has also been recognised by large and small dictatorships, with the resultant suppression of art, either directly or indirectly. Indirect suppression takes the form of withholding support financially for the proverbially impoverished artist, whose love of their chosen medium is so consuming a passion that they would rather starve than fight.

One of the most graphic and well-known pieces of art that depicts the artist's political Resistance, is Picasso's "Guernica". Here the images in their grotesque postures, writhe in the aftermath of the Spanish civil war, their horrors displayed for all the world to witness. No words are needed. The images say it all in one space and time.

Van Gogh painted out his Resistance to his own inner journey, his rage and torment smeared exquisitely across the canvas. We now love the passion and vibrancy of this direct transferral from his mind to flat surface, without any loss in translation. Another way we can look at his art is to see that it was an expression that had no Resistance – it was the one place where he could witness himself in all his fullness.

MUSIC

For the musician, and composer, Resistance can be expressed in so many ways. Through words in songs, through the quality of sounds, we hear and respond - sometimes sympathetically, sometimes not. Maybe it brings up our own Resistance to what is being said or implied. Maybe it jangles our sensitive ears and minds. Maybe it takes us to the heavens, like Mozart's music might do. The use of dissonance in music composition immediately conveys Resistance and its accompanying disharmony; yet the triumph after the struggle always resolves the melody.

Songs of freedom that stand the test of time, are usually the ones that are gentler, that have a sense of surrender, that have lost their anger in the fight. Such as the 'classic' songs 'Blowing in the Wind' by Dylan, or 'Redemption Song' by Marley. On a more peaceful front, the Negro Spiritual and Gospel Songs were sung to raise spirits in difficult times, and used as a means of bringing 'heart' into their form of Resistance, to help give them endurance in their situation.

The books and trainings of Tim Gallwey help musicians (as well as sports people) conquer areas of mental Resistance in the pursuit of excellence in their art.

'Fear and over-control do not produce the best players, they are also likely to inhibit the production of good music'   Gallwey

'Too much challenge, not enough safety, leads to stress;
Too little challenge, too much safety, leads to boredom'   Gallwey

THEATRE

Although theatre is well-known for its part in conveying Resistance in a counter-revolutionary context, the art of the actor in finding this place of inner conflict within himself, is profound. We know it when we witness this – the actor is able to convey depth of character, layers of self, which can even 'steal the show' from the more principal actors, for someone with a small part in the play.

Since the most thorough exploration of Resistance and its stages, for the actor, can be found in the book, 'A Director Prepares' by Anne Bogart, it simply remains to quote these best lines direct from her clear observations, in the chapter devoted to Resistance in Theatre. There are too many in-depth quotes that show so much of the value of this process, to leave out:-

(p.137 on) "Since the artist cares in a particular way for the phase of experience in which union is achieved, he does not shun moments of Resistance and tension. He rather cultivates them, not for their own sake but because of their potentialities, bringing to living consciousness an experience that is unified and total..."
Resistance heightens and magnifies the effort.
'Every act generates Resistance to that act. To sit down to write almost always requires a personal struggle against the
Resistance to write...'
Entropy and inertia are the norm. To meet and overcome Resistance is a heroic act that requires courage, and a connection to a
reason for the action ...'
"Our struggle to create ... is a fight against the weight and slowness of our own decay...(Art) rises above the Resistance against it.
Recognise that Resistances that present themselves will immediately intensify your commitment and generate energy in the endeavour
Resistance demands thought, provokes curiosity and mindful alertness – and when overcome and utilized, eventuates in elation.
Ultimately the quality of any work is reflected in the size of
obstacles encountered."
'If one's attitude is right, joy vigour and break-throughs will be the results of Resistance met rather than avoided'
'The calibre of the obstacle determines the quality of the expression.
If there are not enough obstacles in a given process, the result can lack rigour and depth.
Meeting a Resistance, confronting an obstacle, or over-coming a difficulty, always demands creativity and intuition.'
'In the heat of the conflict, you have to call on new reserves of energy and imagination.'
You develop your muscles in the act of overcoming Resistance ...
'The magnitude of the Resistance you choose to engage determines the progression and depth of your work. The larger the obstacles,
the more you will transform in the effort'
An artist learns to concentrate rather than get rid of the daily discord and restlessness. It is possible to turn the irritating mass of daily frustrations into fuel for beautiful expression.
"But in moments of discord and discomfort, in the instant that we feel challenged by the circumstances, our natural inclination is to stop. Don't stop. Try to allow for the necessary discomfort generated by the struggle with the present circumstances.
Use this discomfort as a stimulus for expression by concentrating it."

There is no expression without excitement, without turmoil.
But where there is no shaping of materials in the interest of embodying the excitement / discomfort, there is no self-expression only self-exposure and discharge.
Meet the challenge of discomfort.
Compression makes expression possible...– a problem channelled with maturity and value.
Expression is the result of containing, shaping and embodying excitement that boils up inside of you.
I can splatter my feelings around the room, or I can concentrate them and let them cook until the appropriate moment in which I might express an opinion or sentiment.
The actor has to build a sense of conflict or Resistance in the body

Laziness	*3 very real enemies = 3 constant Resistances that we face in almost every moment of our waking life -*
Impatience	*The challenge is to think and to act how we handle these 3 real enemies*
Distraction	*determines the clarity and force of our achievements.*

Distraction is an external energy. The temptation to be diverted by outside stimulus is an obstacle to be found everywhere ...we are encouraged to switch channels, shop, cruise by, surf, call someone or take a break.
Attitude is the key. Naming something as a problem engenders the wrong relationship with it.
It predetermines a pessimistic already-defeated attitude....
Start with a forgiving relationship to laziness and impatience, and cultivate a sense of humour about them both (L and I) and then trick them with timing of projects and readiness.
Encounters with Resistance and the compression of emotion, generate one of the most crucial conditions for the theatre: energy....The opposition between a force pushing towards action and another force holding back, is translated into visible and feel-able energy in space and time. This personal struggle with the obstacle in turn induces discord and imbalance.
The attempt to restore harmony from this agitated state generates yet more energy.
It is natural and human to seek union and restore balance from the imbalance of engagement with discord. [eg: Shakespeare soliloquy while standing on one leg – suddenly the body speaks with astonishing clarity and necessity.
This battle is, in itself, a creative act.
Paradoxically, you cultivate Resistance in order to free your path of Resistance.
You welcome obstacles in order to find a way to annihilate them.
The object is freedom.
The result is freedom too.

FILM

What an extra-ordinary medium the one of Film is! What an opportunity we have, to convey absolutely anything to so many people. This fact has thankfully been seized by most of the currently suppressed peoples of the world. Even though few cinemas show many World Cinema pieces, those of us who hear along the 'grapevine' will be able to find these movies.

There have been profoundly moving stories built up around personal narrative within such a context. Examples are 'The Kite Runner' – set in the Afghanistan of the Taliban and in the USA, and movies actually smuggled out from Tibet – and 'Hotel Rwanda.' There are probably already new films that are also coming out of Iraq since the war/s. The power of Resistance movements comes out most strongly once again, when the story is told without denial, but also without attack – where the facts and what we observe speak volumes, even though the horror of what we are witnessing is almost unbearable to watch.

THE WRITTEN WORD

The easiest way to disseminate controversial material is through the written word. This is why, historically, one of the first things to be destroyed or manipulated, by incoming regimes, is the newspapers and their printing technology.

Samson Destroys the Temple
by Julius Schnoor von Carolsfeld,
The 19th Century wood engraver

We are possibly much more influenced by other people's words than by any other means of communication. They form the basis of our understanding of the world. So much so, that we often don't even believe our own eyes. There is a large volume of documented evidence of this, usually in the realm of psychology – whereby a series of questions asked of a witness shifts their view of reality until they believe the altered suggestion. It takes a very strong mind indeed, to Resist such influence, in order to trust one's own wisdom and observation.

ARCHITECTURE, BOATS and GARDENS

This section simply outlines the other important, but mostly self-explanatory, aspects of our world that actually benefit from the use of Resistance.

Whether with functional or innovative architecture, Resistance has to be not only taken into account, but is also a vital factor in creating 3D structures that stay standing! Walls need to Resist or withstand gravity – building materials need to Resist decay, and the effects of time and the elements. Metals need to be stress-Resistant. Furniture materials need to be fire-Resistant.

Such considerations are the same with boats and their need for water-Resistance, in the face of severe weather conditions.

Landscape designers can also allow for plants that support each others' natural pest Resistance. Plant Resistance is similar to innate immunity in animals, in that it is acquired from an attack on one part of the plant, inducing Resistance in the whole. It requires the accumulation of the plant hormone salicylic acid (Latin for willow tree), similar to the active component of aspirin. Finally, trees need to yield as they Resist strong winds, rain and drought.

FENG SHUI

Feng Shui works with Resistance and turns it around, so that it works for us. A purpose of the interesting study of Feng Shui, is to find ways to allow the flow of energy, that will help aspects of our lives function more fluently.

Although the language of Feng Shui is rather strange to us Westerners – couched as it is in the ancient Chinese way of seeing the world – there are some fundamental archetypal truths in it. This is why we can understand it.

Even though we do not see our world as 'sending daggers into us' from odd corners of buildings, inside or out, we do see the point of this understanding of energy flow. The intention is to allow free and supportive flow of energy – it could even be that air-flow is improved in our surroundings and this would be conducive to clearer thinking.

If we Resist de-cluttering our space, what is it that we are Resisting? Of course there is one lovely way of allowing space to de-clutter itself: leave it all alone, and let the moths and mice nibble away quietly and make their nests in it. Nature always and eventually reclaims everything.

So the Resistance is to "letting go", always. Letting go of aspects of the past, a person or people, situations, even our wonderful and eternally memorable travels. The Resistance may also be in the form of an attachment to the future –

what shall I leave my children / friends, to show them who I really am (was)? This is also an aspect of the ego — how we present ourselves, where our mind and consciousness really is, how we wish to be seen.

This art of Feng Shui also encourages discernment: the essential balance of trust and wisdom, whereby you can trust (Allah), but should also tie up your camel — to mix cultures. In other words, it is in many ways a very practical study — for example, why sit with our back to the door, when any moment of absence of mind or concentration can allow surprise and possible upset?

Feng Shui uses different aspects of creative life to support free-flow: Mirrors, to reflect possible negative energy or thoughts back where they came from; Colours to change the environmental vibration; homage to Higher Beings, in the form of pictures that raise one's gratitude. Gentle sounds that raise one's thought patterns. Water-features to encourage flow and release. All these enhancements of the environment serve to raise our spirits, which we need in our stressful lives.

The ART of MULES

Finally, and in the lighter spirit that our Eeyore is somehow capable of creating, here are a few samples of that very important field of Mules in art and music.

"Miles of Mules" was a public art project, which placed hundreds of life-size fiberglass mules, decorated by local area artists, in parts of the USA in the summer of 2003. This would counter the gorgeously painted cows that circulated (moooved around ?) New Zealand and Australia in the early 2000's.

Tom Waits' "Mule Variations' — especially 'Get behind the Mule'

'Muleskinner Blues' — sung with amazing yodels, by the confident labourer seeking work ("I can make any mule listen,

Or I won't accept your pay, Hey hey")

Mule Music   'Don't step on my blue-suede mules…?!'

Chapter 10 - Teenagers and Resistance

Of: Rebellion and Butterflies

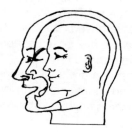

The 3 Faces of Harry:-

The Mask of 'Harry Cool'

The Shadow of 'Dirty Harry'

The Core is 'HARRY KRISHNA'

Thanks to Jo May, group facilitator, Lamorna Cornwall, 1984
(Drawing by CCJ)
'Even the desert holds within it the promise of beautiful life –
yet it still needs the rain to make it bloom'   Prem Rawat

PARENTS EYE VIEW

It is often said that we wish there was an Instruction Manual for Life, and certainly for bringing up children. All we have to go on is what we were taught directly or indirectly by our parents, for better or worse. Then we either copy them because it makes sense, or because we find that, somehow, we cannot help ourselves acting the very way we hated being treated. Or else we make huge efforts to change the way we witnessed parenting first hand, swearing to ourselves 'I will never do that to my children' – and possibly even swing the other way entirely. Then perhaps the pendulum swing is 'too great' and we over-compensate.

This whole attempt to change the manner of parenting is an expression of our own Resistance to our parents' way of doing this most important of occupations. And yet, here in this western way of isolation, with so little community support, we are having to re-invent the wheel with each new generation. In this context, our own natural rebellion is expressed as Resistance to what we see around us – whether we think it doesn't 'work', or that it has so many constraints that we wish to break away from, and we attempt to create a whole new way of being and parenting.

This is where rebellion and Resistance can be constructive. Surely there must be a purpose in changing everything, and challenging the status quo by initiating Resistance to change. When we are in the centre of chaos around us, in the maelstrom of great change, the purpose of stirring it all up would be to loosen the old structures. The best description of the value of chaos, is of the glass of water, with mud that has compacted at the bottom of the glass, which is then so stirred up by the addition of pure new water, that it looks as if it is altogether muddy. Of course, the solution (pardon the pun) is to continue pouring in pure water, until the mud finally clears. That's when it becomes clear that it was worth 'hanging on in there.'

SOCIETY

In fact, our teenagers are directly and indirectly challenging our cherished beliefs about how the world should be run. And if they are not doing that, they are reflecting and pointing out those things that do need to change. They do this by highlighting the failures in our society and by acting out the very weak spots in the way we want our world to be. It's like poking a wound, scratching at a scab because it is imperfect. And they will continue to scratch until we make those changes.

What are those changes that we of the older generation are so Resistant to make? Some of the changes include the need to spend more time with our offspring, no matter how 'grungy' they can be. They are teaching us, by pushing us into *unconditional love*.

We have to remain there, available to them, for the time that they do turn to us, or are ready to divulge what is happening in their world.

In a way, what begins to happen, usually from puberty, is that the children increasingly claim their own timing in all matters. We become so used to calling the shots in terms of getting the children ready to go out, coming in for meals, and being asked for a report on how they are doing at school or other events. Then they begin to say 'no' more and more – unless they are being 'good', in order to please us – but then in this case the rebellion may come out in other, possibly more obscure, ways.

This is when we need to shift the tables more, and allow them their sense of timing, while still holding the 'norm' for them to bounce off. Consistency is the hardest thing to maintain, in the face of their rage and their struggling to create a personalised identity – this is rather like holding a drowning person above the water's power. But it has to be done.

There is an element of T'ai Chi in this whole process. That is, to allow the Resistance its full expression, which then burns itself out and resolves itself naturally into a much clearer picture. This is the picture that can then be worked with, to enable it to be a success for everybody involved, while negotiating a path through the tricky new land. This assumes that we are prepared to listen to what they have to say, and that they themselves have something different to add to what the family is 'saying', in its 'life of quiet desperation' (Thoreau).

Simon Drew www.simondrew.co.uk

COMMUNICATION

The main way we demonstrate our Resistance to hearing what they have to say, is by blocking communication. We do this by any of the following means, all of which are forms of moral table tennis, whereby we control the ball and make sure it never stays on our side of the net:-

a. Undermining / Judging / Lecturing / Giving advice / Ridiculing / Diagnosing / Moralising / Interrogating - making the other feel small, in order to feel big, and avoid the issue;

b. Controlling / Ordering / Warning – these more aggressive forms of control are very suppressing for even the strongest person, and enable the aggressor to have the 'high ground' but lose the inner fight;

c. Sympathising   This is in its own category, since when carried out in an over-bearing way, can be stifling and have the effect of blocking the other's speech

The first 2 are used when giving 'consequences' as a form of punishment and pain, as opposed to a solution-focused means of conveying our reasons for setting boundaries.

TEENAGERS'-EYE-VIEW

What are our adolescents Resisting? Change. From within, this time. As the new hormones kick in, a chemical maelstrom shifts everything in sight, and also out of sight. Bodies change shape, things get bigger, and so does every conceivable emotion. But, depending on the childhood relationship with emotions, the newly emerging adult handles their ever-shifting emotions well, or not so well.

The wave of disturbing and rapidly shifting sands of uncertainty can knock anyone over, and they do, regularly – but not regularly enough to allow the adolescent to be prepared for this turmoil.

The recalcitrant teenager begins to discover what life actually means to him and how many of his values may differ from those of the rest of the family. The disobedience is his way of claiming the space to do that. So also is the power inherent in Passive Resistance, where apparent disinterest will get him what he wants.

There is a similarity with the journey of a Butterfly. The cute but voracious caterpillar hides away – probably doesn't wash for weeks – as it melts and dissolves into a goo in its chrysalis. But if left alone, with respect for its process, it breaks out of its apparent prison, metamorphosing in order to emerge as the beautiful healthy adult it was always destined to be.

However, for some, along with these changes comes shame and, therefore, the need to hide and cover up. And this cover up is usually a coping mechanism for dealing with the overwhelming nature of this emotional 'sandblast.' The coping mechanisms used can cause them to turn to our modern 'teenage culture', of sex, drugs, and rock'n'roll or to immerse themselves in the computer world of the internet, games or, ideally, they may turn to some form of creativity. One way or the other, this is when and how they somehow learn to cope with their new inner world, which cannot be avoided – it seems to be the traitor from within that has come to permanently disturb our sometimes cosy view of the world, especially that of our families.

SUPPORT

How can we as adults help in this fearful transition? Really the only way is to simply be there, be the rock against which their pounding seas can batter and come and go. That is without being inhuman ourselves – where we might be tempted to deny our own failings, which of course continue to be the grist for our own personal mill.

It is also very important to try to maintain communication – without endlessly asking where they are at. This may be an especially good time to disclose some of our own failings, how we dealt with them and in what way we were successful. Showing how we learned from our mistakes is as valuable as 'doing it right' at the outset – possibly more so.

As far as the sex and drug culture is concerned, this is potentially a mine-field for all parties. This is where we really do have to remember our own adolescence, and the deep urge to explore. The most helpful thing we can do is to pave the way for a 'look-before-you-leap' mentality. Safe sex and clear information about drugs is THE way to go. We cannot be prescriptive about the age at which our children do these things, because they are jolly-well going to do it if and when they choose. That is part of the necessity of rebellion, and their Resistance to 'the way it's always been done.'

Let's just make sure they know in advance what the possible consequences are, from each possible action.

We don't need to give full sex-education to them – that should be happening at school, and they probably know plenty from their friends. Perhaps they should know that if there's anything that really doesn't make sense, they should ask, privately, for advice from a teacher, or a friend who has nothing much to prove but has some common sense.

In the drugs world, the most important thing they should know is to ask if something is *strong*. To listen out for the phrase 'this is excellent stuff' – which probably means it's very strong, and may have been genetically modified by the growers (especially the stuff called 'skunk' in the marijuana world), or laced with something like opium or speed. They should be encouraged to be careful who they accept drinks from, no matter how tempting it may be to accept a 'free' drink at a bar, and how nice it is to feel that one is attractive to a stranger. If they have any suspicions, they can simply appear to drink the offering, drop it or devise something inventive to avoid drinking it.

And if, with all the best will in the world, and all this preparation, something serious does go wrong, it will be very clear that you are both / all about to embark on an intense growing journey. This is where we need to gather as much help as we can from all corners, including our parents and older folk, whether we have Resistance to that or not. They may or may not have experience in this particular field, but they hold a perspective, which we need to allow them to demonstrate for us.

The worst-case scenario is that, regular use of any potent drugs may bombard the immune system so much, and 'sand-blast' the social mask so much, that they are left feeling raw and exposed and stuck in a frozen state in this part of their evolution. All that can be done here is to don your 'endurance' cloak, and find assistance in whatever form works for you. This may be in the form of a strong individual shoulder – but ideally in groups so the load is shared and you allow yourself the journey that is needed. This journey is truly what we are all here to do. See Chapters 14 and 15 for more detail.

THE WAY OF THE ASS

In a way, the journey of the adolescent can be likened to the 'Way of the Ass.' Here, the lessons learned have to be achieved through the proverbial 'falling on one's ass' (and hoping the ass then continues to carry them forward, as they lie comatose across its back). Yet this seems to be the only way of really learning our lessons – by trying out our own versions of the actions performed by our parents. If our teenagers can follow this path, and not succumb to the fears and accusations of onlookers, but even find a way to laugh at themselves, then their future will be the brightest of all. They will soon learn not to make too much of an ass of themselves, or to take to heart those times when they do. And let's not take it too personally when they make 'assinine' comments !

'Mules tend to be very attention-seeking, and ignoring them for bad behavior and praising them for good behavior works very well on youngsters.'

This is applied to 'good mule husbandry', but there is no reason it can't be applied to our youngsters. The trick is to fall on one's ass, then get up and carry on, without fear of making an ass of oneself.

OVERVIEW

Always, our teenagers are our teachers of course – they show up those places in ourselves where we need to move on, to loosen up and let go, to show up our own weaknesses. Basically they highlight our own Resistances, as well as witnessing their own. But it is a new journey for them, where we older ones at least have had some practice at handling or coping with those emotional spaces. Whether we have used that time wisely, is another matter – but then we ourselves get bowled over by emotional tornados that seem to arrive unannounced, and we have to deal with them too. That includes our own reactions to our teenagers' journeys, which come from our own unresolved issues and the Resistance to our own full journey.

All the observations above can of course be applied to any relationships and the inevitable issues that are encountered, at all ages.

Just when we thought it was comfortable to be in this world, 'they' come along and stir it all up for us.

Section B:-
RESISTANCE in the INNER, META-PHYSICAL WORLD
Here, our 'hero' has miraculously mule-tated to a Human Being,
and begins his 'inner' journey.

Chapter 11 – Resistance to Change

Of: Motion and Emotion
Breatharians and Manna,
Fear and accidents and 12 Steps

"Knowledge is power." Francis Bacon
"WHAT YOU RESIST, PERSISTS" Carl Jung
'There is only FEAR or LOVE' A Course in Miracles
This too shall pass - רובעי הז מג *(Hebrew: gam zeh ya'avor)*
- an expression passed on to Solomon
Resistance blocks motion and creates emotion - CCJ
"We have met the enemy and he is us" - Pogo in
'Waiting for Godot' by Beckett)

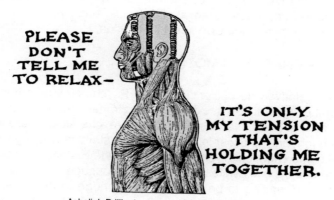

PLEASE
DON'T
TELL ME
TO RELAX –

IT'S ONLY
MY TENSION
THAT'S
HOLDING ME
TOGETHER.

Asheligh Brilliant   www.ashleighbrilliant.com

MOTION and EMOTION

Travelling through life we are in motion. Since energy cannot be created or destroyed, there must be a 'life-times' worth of energy that propels us into birth and beyond. Or perhaps our 'supplies' (our 'daily bread' or Manna) arrive with every in-breath. The Vedic ancients called this 'Prana' and there are some today who claim they can last for many days - a rare few for months (some claim for years) on fresh air alone ('Breatharians'). And then toxic discharge is released with every out-breath.

Energy is constantly changing form. If Divine Prana – or Manna from 'heaven' is constantly being given from Source with every Breath (after all, the sun shines on all without judgement or pre-conditions), what is it that we are mostly 'giving back'? What happens to that pure energy?

PHYSICAL MOTION

Physically speaking, it is well known that air is 20% oxygen and 78% nitrogen and other minor gases. It is inhaled, from that first inhaled breath onwards, and the cycle begins. The respiratory centres in the brain, located around the 4th Ventricle in the back of the brain (and above the cerebellum) stimulate the respiratory muscles, especially the diaphragm, to contract. The inhaled air is drawn into the alveoli, the grape-like air sacs of cells at the end of the bronchioles. At a cellular level, the oxygen diffuses across the cell walls, while carbon dioxide, CO_2 is exchanged ready to be exhaled. The oxygen enters the blood stream, binding with haemoglobin in the red blood cells, and is carried around the body to nourish every cell (ideally). Meanwhile the CO_2 is exhaled, partially by small muscle contraction, but mostly by the elastic recoil of the lungs. This continues until the last breath is exhaled at life's end.

When we express ourselves, we use muscles, in true 'Mediterranean style' with full manual gesticulations, or simply with our vocal chords, our facial expressions, or a rare few of us can express 'multiverses' (thinking of Stephen Hawking) with the blink of an eye. The muscles require good nerve supply, good circulatory supply and waste removal of the lactic acid by-products of use.

They also need their own specific nutrition.

EMOTION as ENERGY IN MOTION

In the relatively new science of PNI – Psycho-Neuro-Immunology, it is now accepted that every emotion has its own neurotransmitter that can be fabricated in every cell of the body. Neurotransmitters are chemical secretions that were originally thought only to occur in the Nervous system, conveying vital information. Then these same chemicals were discovered in the Endocrine (glandular) system, then the Immune system (white blood cells, macrophages), then all cells. It is either 'there' in the cell waiting to be 'needed' as a bridge to the transmission of this information to every other cell - or it is made up of the building blocks of the protein-based enzymes that are present for the purpose of other more functional communications (Chopra).

In other words, no sooner has an emotion been stirred up by an event, or a thought (also performed under laboratory conditions), but a whole new stream of neurotransmitter communication affects every cell in the whole body. Some neurotransmitters known to non-scientists, are: Serotonin, Opiates, and Dopamine.

Emotionally we are only beginning to understand how deeply we are all affected in life, and how this aspect of ourselves is the mark of our humanity - namely, to be able to feel. We are also seeing how directly our emotions are linked with the manner in which we breathe. These days this observation appears to be common knowledge, so that many types of therapist exhort us to 'Breathe!' when we appear to be holding on to our feelings, because holding the breath seems to stop the motion of emotion.

REASONS for RESISTING CHANGE

Although the original cause of Resisting change lies back in the dawn of time, when tribal cohesion kept the wolf from the door, change itself has always been with us. It is the process by which we learn and evolve. But we have always carried fear of change. The first potentially memorable change is Birth itself. Leaving the warm, soft and nourished environment for a cold, dangerous and helpless state, is the ultimate and first change we have all experienced. Depending on just how cold and dangerous we perceived or experienced it to be, this experience will affect our life-long expectations of how life will handle us, and how we will handle life.

Fear itself is based on pain, survival and pain-avoidance, whether physical, mental, emotional or spiritual. And we are all subject to different levels of fear, which we have to learn to deal with on a daily basis. This is the 'human condition', or one way to see it.

There are different emotional fears that reflect our Resistance:-
Fear of disapproval and ridicule from parents, family, friends, society
Fear of being a 'tall poppy' in society, and 'risking our necks'
Fear of acknowledging and feeling our emotions
Fear of letting go of those emotions, and experiencing the love beneath them (because that would make us 'wrong');
More specifically, we can have fears of:
Letting go of anger or rage – Resistance to finding a solution for both parties
Letting go of grief and sadness: Resistance to the next step and finding one's own life continuing after the death of a loved one, death of a relationship – or maybe the grief hasn't been expressed to its real depth. Once again, through fear of letting go and losing control, a fear that one would be unable to 'come out the other side' of the emotion – that perhaps there isn't 'another side';
Letting go of control, since we may have to surrender to the flow of life. We all know people (including ourselves) who show rigidity in response to life's changes.

Sometimes change feels like a huge wall of difficulty that has to be scaled or toppled or run from. It has been likened to meeting a tiger, and standing frozen with fear, waiting for the tiger to jump at our throats. However, if you wait a little, it becomes clear that it is a paper tiger that looks impossibly real. If you dare to advance, and watch its lack of movement, you will be able to pierce its heart, and continue along your path. But you have to have the courage to take that first step.

CHANGE FEELS GOOD

Imagine the other extreme – nothing changing. This would be so intensely boring. Imagine only rain, or only sun with the same very hot temperature all year round. We couldn't bear it for a whole lifetime, although we would adapt. So in all honesty, change does feel good. It brings up challenges, so is stimulating and interesting. And as we all know, we certainly live in 'interesting' times, true to the Chinese curse. Conversely, when only change is happening, we are drained beyond belief, and pray for stillness in the tornado of movement, for at least a whistle-stop in the Eye of the Storm.

Change allows room for adventure and inspiration, learning, understanding and joy. The security that comes from hanging on to comfort is illusory, and change will be forced upon one by life's circumstances, in order to make us grow.

WHAT YOU RESIST PERSISTS

Carl Jung brought us this powerful understanding of energy and Resistance. What it means is that, the very act of pushing away either a feeling or a change, will cause it to not only stay around for longer, but even cause it to expand. It creates a Resistance loop that draws us around and around, until we are desperately seeking a way out, a way to run away from the pain of that feeling, of that memory. The need to confront that 'paper tiger' (which certainly does not feel like paper at the time, the illusion is so strong) is the only way to release ourselves from the strangling effect of the effort involved in avoiding the pain of looking at it.

This defended stance, which may sometimes be sheer obstinacy, is likely to build up into an emotional or physical shock of some sort that may appear to that person to have come from nowhere. Although with the clarity of hindsight, the prelude to the 'fall' may have been visible all along, but may have been too scary to consider, and too large to prevent.

It is as if the act of focusing energy, so that it actually becomes intention and attention on that thing that is being avoided, gives it a little more strength. The purpose for this cruel universal law is in order for us to consciously heal that wound. If we could successfully place the offending fearful memory in a drawer somewhere, in a derelict house, we would never look at it, and it would never heal. It demands attention until it is healed.

SOLUTION

You have to discover what it is that's bringing something towards you, and break out of the Resistance Loop. You have to either do what you are Resisting - or not.

But finally, if your base-line / root Intention is for the Highest, you cannot fail. Ultimately it is only Grace that can fully remove the addiction to that form of Resistance and your surrender to that Grace - or to the 'God of your understanding' (the '12 Steps' of Alcoholics Anonymous) that allows it to work. Do whatever helps you to relax into a state of acceptance. If you do not do this, that is OK since it is only a matter of Time in a time-less Universe before you find in yourself, the hunger and thirst to do so.

ACCIDENTS

Narratives abound that tell of people who have miraculously survived severe accidents or illnesses. Almost always the purpose for this severe and life-threatening event becomes clear to all, including themselves. Either it has occurred as a result of the build-up of Resisted awareness, or the discovery of the universal potential for miracles has been an essential next step for that person and their close ones. It is almost as if the energy that was building had to be transformed through a huge event that could not be avoided.

As we go through life, we have repeated opportunities to learn to let go and be fully who we are. We are unconditionally given pure Life energy (élan vital) and have this lifetime to practice following the path of least Resistance. Until then we trip ourselves up, block our emotions or our motion, hurt ourselves or others, and then judge ourselves for it all.

If only there was an easier way to learn than through adversity, and our Resistance to change. Resistance (or lack of it) is often the measure by which we assess our progress along the 'path.'

Would we value our positive experiences so deeply if they came easily? Maybe one day we will.

It is said' 'You can change a fool, but you can't change a Mule.' I hope to show this to be a generalization whose truth is proved by the exceptions. Reading once again through the Limerick at the front, we see how *anybody* can change. But those of us who long to witness that change in someone close to us, will have to step back and allow the Universe to provide the means for change, since 'It' is totally aware of the actual state of the Soul of the 'Mule.'

Chapter 12 - Resistance to Healing

Of: A Course in Miracles;
Forms of Inner Resistance; including Depression,
The 'Death Urge' and Immortality;

'Healing is always certain. It is impossible to let illusions be brought to truth and keep the illusions. Healing will always stand aside when it would be seen as threat. The instant it is welcome, it is there.'
A Course in Miracles – Manual for Teachers - Is Healing Certain?
Resistance is defined as: 'mental forces opposed to self-knowledge'
From Psycho-analytical text
'It is easier to suffer than to act' – Bert Hellinger
'Although the world is full of suffering, it is also full of the overcoming of it.'   Helen Keller
Time is the glue that binds, then releases,
the Resistor & the Resisted   CCJ

It could be said that, if we are alive and on this Earth, we have returned by soul choice, to heal something that needs to be healed. That may be physical, emotional, mental and/or spiritual. Even for those of us who are, or wish to be, teachers, we are by no means 'above this law.' If anything, the spotlight is on us to live and lead by example.

The admonition for the *'Physician (to) heal thyself'* has profound implications. These are not only related to healing physical ailments either – this phrase has mostly been misinterpreted to mean that healers 'should' be healthy. Rather, I believe it concerns depth of healing, whereby the healer needs to journey within himself to meet and integrate his own inner fears and darkness. Herein lies the (understandable) Resistance.

The correlation of Resistance in our inner world is fear. It is said that we are expressing either Love or Fear, in our dualistic Universe. Fear is based on survival, whether real or perceived. And to the one experiencing fear, a perceived threat may as well be real – the same fight / flight / freeze scenario actually occurs within the brain's physiology especially brain-serotonin production (Locke) (and Kiecolt-Glaser in, *'Interpersonal Relationships and Immune Function'*.)

Fear itself is very insidious, and comes cloaked in probably as many forms as there are people on the planet. Because fear is so close to our primal selves, one of the first awakening experiences we usually have is the sudden awareness that a certainty we had in our view of life, comes from a fearful thought. We were so certain that this way of seeing our world was exactly as others would see it, and suddenly it is only our perception that has made it seem so real.

The true teacher stimulates such an awakening, whether by design or by default. That is because they 'walk their talk'. And even the greatest of our teachers are still growing and evolving. It's just that from our lesser perspective, we often cannot see that.

MULISH RESISTANCE

In this chapter, we see the forms of Resistance our Mule puts up, as he yells 'I'm not Resistant' and runs out of the room. Ah, the sweet smell of denial ! It can be so disconcerting for the teacher, who is on her own journey of self-trust and awareness. How to tread carefully and genuinely in the dance of awakening ? It is like Mule-Whispering, where one takes the damaged creature and gently leads him not only back to Trust, but further than he has ever gone before. Yet the fact that the Mule has come this far is such a good sign, since he can never 'un-know' what he has discovered, even if he takes fright and runs for several years. It is only a matter of time before the call to grow, sings too loudly to ignore.

WHAT ARE WE RESISTING?

Ultimately, we are Resisting the truth of our absolute greatness: the highest aspect of ourselves that is self-healing and self-regenerating. For many, herein lies a conflict of belief. This statement implies that God who is 'The Greatest' has no place in this 'ego-centric' model. However, this view shows that the most fundamental message from all forms of sacred writings, has not been understood: namely that we are ALL sons and daughters of God, made in his/her own image (the Divine hologram).

We are not separate from God, and never have been. This belief or thought of separation is the first and greatest illusion that was birthed in the 'Fall of Man'. It may be seen to be reflected in the actual process of birth, where we have to be separated from our Goddess / mother in order to survive physically. Our first Breath, and the cutting of the umbilical cord, propels us into our independence and our seeming separation. And it is often the first deeply painful experience that we have to endure alone.

Looking at what makes us Resist, or avoid accepting this Truth, we see that what we are usually motivated by, is the avoidance and fear of pain. In the human experience, pain hurts, and in a survival consciousness, we will often go the long way round, until the need for confrontation of the apparent source of pain cannot be avoided any longer. We hereby acquiesce to Time to provide the circumstances of our confrontation, and our healing. Many on Earth understand this.

Fakirs (religious devotees) of physical self-mastery take themselves through rituals of facing their pain consciously, and acting out self-wounding. But the ritual itself summons up the workings of endorphins that may even make the normally painful process pleasurable. In addition, where this is done repeatedly over time, there may be a level of dissociation, where the pain is felt to be occurring outside the body, or depersonalised.

This dissociation is what occurs for people when a painful event has arrived without conscious choice, and this often becomes the coping strategy. The memory is locked away in a part of the body-mind until, or if, it is safe to find a way to look at it. This process of 'unfreezing' painful memories is, beautifully and sensitively explored, in the books by Levene and Mindell.

THOUGHT IS CREATIVE

Most of us Resist the related and fundamental Truth – that Thought is Creative. The understanding of this comes from the awareness that our thoughts, whether conscious or (mostly) unconscious are the source of our reality. If, from an aspect of our birth, and probably pre-birth, we witness our mother's pain – we are likely to believe we cause others / women, pain. Or if the male Obstetrician is rough in handling us: that others / men, cause us pain. This is the basic tenet of the Rebirthing-Breathwork model – that the journey to full self-responsibility must involve looking at the thoughts and beliefs that have arisen from our earliest and pre-verbal experiences. This is the source of our Resistance to change: the view that 'life is hard and then you die'. Birth is the second huge change to our Souls; the arrival of the Soul into an embryo or foetus is the first enormous change to our energy-state, as we 'descend' into Matter.

One of the results of any of our negative thoughts about ourselves, or others, is that we work hard (often unconsciously) to making sure we remain 'right' about this view of ourselves, or others. We will go out of our way to show the world that, it's true. For example: 'the world is really out to get me, the world hurts me or men hurt me' etc. These 'birth-thoughts' (as explained further in Chapter 13), and their possible consequences are great in number, depending on the individuals' experiences. Understanding this process, along with some ways to heal these misconceptions, are all explained in books by Sondra Ray.

This model can and may need to be taken back even further, to before birth itself. The greatest self-responsibility comes from the acceptance that, for reasons we often confront on our journey, we actually choose our parents. This of course assumes that we were already a conscious being, or at least were being guided by conscious beings, in the pre-life dimensions. If anyone has difficulty with the idea that there is a before-and-after-life invisible realm, it would be wise to look at the basic law of physics, concerning Energy: namely that *Energy cannot be created or destroyed*. It can only be changed, transformed and transmuted.

If that is the case, then from our pre-birth moment of choice, we make 'Sacred Contracts' (Myss) with certain people, family or others, to augment our personal evolution. These people either teach us directly, or they provide conflicts for us to resolve and heal. We may also make a sacred contract with ourselves, that if, by a certain age or stage, we have not learned what we have come to learn, that we might manifest an accident or illness that will shift us the most.

THE CAN OF WORMS

One gruesome analogy that has come to me is an exploration of the proverbial and infamous imagery of the 'can of worms' – namely, our inner 'shadows'. We all have them. There are 3 possible choices as we consider the 'can', remembering it is chained to us, so there is no option to somehow 'eject' it. If we choose the high intention path of spiritual pursuits, without actually examining the worms, it is like opening the lid and then sitting on it, hoping the worms will never see the light of day. However, even the small amount of light that enters is enough for the worms to start to spill out, and everyone gets to see them, but slowly. And I do believe they leave the can for good once they've crawled out, if an honest intention is maintained.

Or we can choose the path of sweet ignor-ance, and drag it around everywhere with us, hoping no-one will notice it clanging and bouncing behind us. However, the worms are programmed to breed if not attended to, and the can will begin to bulge as the worms propagate. Finally they will explode, splattering debris all around us. The good news about this option is that, once exploded and cleaned up, there are a lot fewer worms remaining – however the repercussions of the collateral damage include the possibility of a lifetime's karmic clean-up.

The brave person's choice finally, is to carefully extract one worm at a time, say 'hello', examine it and 'own' it, and then let it go to have a normal worm-life. The trick is to truly let it go. This takes time, but eventually leaves you with a beautiful 'can', with which you can be very creative – witness the million and one useful objects made in Africa out of old tin cans imaginatively recycled.

THE MOMENT OF RESISTANCE

There is a moment of Resistance – a point in time when we decide (usually unconsciously) to Resist. When we experience something, anything, there is always a crossroads: **choice**. Apart from whether to go ahead with this thing to do, or with this thought, there is also the decision as to whether to "judge" the event as 'good' or 'bad'. This is a survival technique, a shortcut to fight or flight. But we tend to apply it to everything, even when there is no actual danger. That is because the event or the words chosen have an element which reminds us of a time, which we justifiably associate with pain, relative to a trauma that did occur for us.

The words spoken are immediately channelled into a sort of 'work station' where they are labelled as being from the same threatening factory, and filed away in a safe box – they may even be put in the deep-freeze where the really painful things have been stored. When one is attempting to live a conscious life, these automatic actions need to be broken down, before they can be stopped and reversed.

BURSTING the BUBBLE of RESISTANCE

This is how we seem to learn – through adversity. It cannot be avoided - it appears to be a law of the Universe. If we imagine our Resistance-to-change as being dragged through life, kicking and screaming, we will see that there is a large amount of energy being channelled into that act of avoidance. This is a huge amount of Potential Energy – energy that can be used to create motion, and light, and the things we truly want and need in our lives. It is effectively locked up in this Resistance – a Black Hole of negative creativity, drawing people, events and objects into its gravitational field.

Taking the idea from Physics, that a Black Hole is at first an apparently negative force field that all things fall into – and transcribing this to an image of our Resistance – we can also see that at its most dense stage, it is a potential galaxy of beauty. This may explain how we sometimes see someone undergoing a huge transformation, when they suddenly encounter a life-threatening situation.

It is as if the bubble of Resistance has been burst by this event. The illusion that has kept that person's life being so difficult is explosively dissolved. It is this potential energy locked up in our Resistance that needs to be honoured. It is actually a creative force for good on its release, at exactly the right moment in time - chosen only by the Soul of each person. The expansion and transformation is beautiful to behold, and is truly awe-inspiring. Watching the many Oprah Winfrey Show descriptions of such transformations, and expansion through intense adversity, we feel truly inspired.

How are you feeling today?

FORMS OF RESISTANCE

There are the many and glorious ways we defend ourselves, as we approach uncomfortable areas. Defensiveness is the way in which others can spot our Resistance. Clues, shall we say? This is not to make us feel self-conscious, but as an aid to being more self-aware. We have to be so careful not to point out others' Resistance in a way that makes us look superior – it is good to remind ourselves that when one points a finger, the other 3 fingers are pointing back to ourselves.

1.   Pointing the finger ! Blame (of self or others):

This is a way we avoid taking responsibility for what we have created in our lives, by 'passing the buck' to the object of our blame. The phrase that is linked with this strategy is: you / he / she made me do it, and the famous Bart Simpson line: 'It wasn't me!' when we all know it was. Also, 'pointing the finger' is how we show that we believe we are not all connected – that we see the source of 'the problem' as being 'out there', as if 'you' were not a part of 'me';

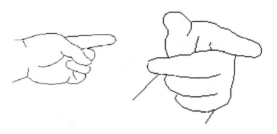

2.   Guilt

In the sense of indicating where our Resistance lies, it is the Resistance of denying our true and total innocence, which is our true nature. From the perspective of our highest, we are ALL doing our best, and any unconsciously performed act may be our way of doing our best under stress. This stress may come from the outside – the need to make a quick decision for example. But usually the stress that causes us to do things we come to regret, emerges from the inside of our minds. It emerges from our negative view of ourselves that drives us to create a situation that we then eventually have to come to forgive of ourselves;

3.   Arguing

'I'm not angry' we yell, stamping our foot in an echo of a childish tantrum. This is the action of Resisting a truth about ourselves that is uncomfortable to hear. This form of Resistance usually comes with very good 'reasons' for not following through and exploring this new awareness of ourselves;

4.   Not listening

Sometimes a truth is spoken directly by someone speaking to us, whose observation causes us discomfort. They can be phrasing it so carefully so as not to hurt more than necessary, but we still close our ears and only hear our own self-judgements. We may never stop long enough to truly listen to hear what could be of value to us.

At other times, a stranger may drop a gem of a clue that would help us, if we would only stop running so fast. That can extend to any number of synchronous events, which show us how connected we all are. We could walk past a shop with our favourite inspiring song playing, or a bus could drive past with an encouraging message that, on the surface, appears to have nothing to do with our current situation. So if we aren't listening (or watching) we will miss it. Sometimes these reminders come through birdsong, or interactions with animals that we have less Resistance to than people.

5.   Sabotage

There may be something greatly desired, like an exciting new job. A mixture of self-doubt and a Resistance to achieving that goal, as it would disprove those negative beliefs, can cause us to sabotage its attainment.

We fluff the interview, turn up late, say the wrong thing to the wrong person, lose the train ticket and spill the carefully chosen healthy yoghurt drink down our best interview clothes. And on top of that, we fail to see the humour in it all. Here, perhaps the Resistance is to the expansion that could result from achievement and the fear of being able to sustain the improved situation. 'Better the devil you know, than the one you don't know!' – staying as we are is so much more comfortable.

6.   Avoidance

'Just slip out the back, Jack, Make a new plan, Stan ... there are 50 ways to leave your lover' (Paul Simon's song). Once again, the Path of Least Resistance calls to us – at least this aspect of it. The comfy option of avoidance, where we side-step the issue in question when it surfaces, or even physically remove ourselves when the going gets tough, and the not-so-tough go shopping. Avoidance can also take the form of creating an island around ourselves that cannot easily be navigated to. There may be very plausible excuses too – 'I can't come as the dog ate the cat' etc. These are ways in which we create our reasons for not turning up - our excuses.

Another favourite method of avoidance is making jokes. It can make everyone laugh, which is satisfying, but it takes the focus away from the deeper subject.

7.   Run away

See (6) and multiply!

8.   Criticising the teacher

The teacher may in fact be wrong, but setting up a clash of wills does not achieve anything. What is it that the teacher is really stirring up? If she/he is too controversial, making us think outside the square, how does this stretch our comfort zones? If she is too 'boring' perhaps we are Resisting being quiet, being still, being aware only of our voice of judgment. If she is just plain wrong, and we really do know better, then we have to find another way to get our message across.

9.   Body Language:

Crossing arms / legs

Falling asleep – this is a favourite of some of us, and may denote becoming 'ungrounded' and often spoken of as 'going unconscious.'

10. The 'Unconscious Death Urge'

This is a huge subject, belonging mostly to the Rebirthing-Breathwork song of wisdom. The understanding of this most confronting of ideas, has its own birth in the foothills of the Himalayas.

In 1970 an extra-ordinary man appeared – there had been no known record of his birth, and it was said he created his body in a cave beside the Gautama Ganga, a tributary of the sacred river Ganges. His apparent age was that of an 18 year-old youth, and he had a profound effect on everyone who came upon him. His simple title was Babaji, which means 'beloved Father'. It became accepted that he was indeed a reincarnation of the previous Babaji (spoken of in Autobiography of a Yogi) who had left his body not many years before, also in the same geographical area – and of previous others, back though time. He was known as the 'deathless Guru' (Guru meaning 'one who leads from darkness 'gu' to light 'ru') – and at the height of his ministry, left his body in 1984, which really shook up a lot of people. Because it was believed that he was the Immortal Guru, it was assumed he would stay forever, and be the Teacher. Maybe this would have meant few would have motivated themselves from within.

However, because Babaji challenged the age-old belief in ageing and death, his example became a personal challenge: to find those places within ourselves that in many ways seek death, in order to avoid or Resist Life. That 'death' does not need to be a dramatic ending of life – it can happen slowly and daily, chipping away at our enjoyment of life. Many of us will have met people, even those who are happy, who seem to be 'winding down' and talking about their lives relative to their age. Yet they may even have the same length of time ahead of them that they have already lived (namely a 50-year old who may yet live to be 100). What will they do for that long time ahead, if they are already speaking of the effects of age? Where has their youthful zest disappeared to ? What circumstances have knocked the wind out of their sail? Can this be healed so that the blocked energy can be released so that they can enthusiastically embrace life again and live in the eternity of Now?

Through Leonard Orr, who spent time with Babaji, the awareness of this fear of life began to be developed through Breathwork, first in hot water, then in 'dry breathing' sessions in the late 1970's. Then even later came cold water Rebirthing, where ones' survival issues surface, to be integrated through Conscious Connected Breathing.

Many fear being weighed down by the effects of age, like the wearing down of an old engine. It is said that there are a few 'Physical Immortals' that live in remote parts of India, regenerating their bodies for hundreds of years. There are now many people who are embracing the consciousness of Physical Immortality, in terms of daily self-examination, living normal 'householder' lives – some being content with the possibility of simple Longevity, rather than Immortality, which of course can't be measured, by definition. Who knows if or when there is a time after which longevity becomes immortality?

The point for such people is in the intention of doing so, and of confronting their own collection of self-limiting beliefs, which in itself deserves great praise. It is also about honouring and appreciating each other in our lives.

These limiting beliefs are often described as one's Death Urge, or the urge towards death, or a diminishment of the life force in a daily sense.

It manifests as losing our childlike qualities, forgetting to play, to have fun, taking life too seriously, avoiding spending money for fear of not having enough in ones old age; affirming age-related problems – we have 'senior moments' all through life, but just notice them in those terms when we are physically older.

$100 A DAY

This tiredness that sweeps over us, comes from the suppression of the Life Urge, due to a large amount of energy being used to keep a painful memory – or a frightening prospect - out of sight and out of mind. Caroline Myss, refers to the suppression of our self-healing energy in terms of us all having a daily Divine gift of say $100 to spend as we wish. We could be using it to invest in an amazing life for ourselves, and feel like a million bucks. But instead, we spend it on 'keeping the lid on the past' or on situations that offer no returns (e.g. our addictions). This suppression involves a large amount of blocked energy that we could free up with our healing. But it may be too much of a threat, to break through our well-established view of reality, and create a miracle.

This is how we generate depression, by Resisting our 'life-urge' – which may in any moment, be needing to express a socially 'unacceptable' emotion like rage or acute disappointment.

This 'ageism' should not be confused with having proper respect for our natural limitations. It would be foolish to embark on a gruelling travelling journey, when we are not fit, putting our bodies through unnecessary strain when unable to handle such an experience. However, when a longing is so strong that it generates endorphins, which enable us to perform surprising feats of endurance, this is an entirely different situation. This is calling upon the higher aspects of our Being and in turn calls upon the body to respond in kind, and transcend our previous limitations. Sri Chinmoy (from India, living in the West) demonstrated for decades how to go beyond normal physical constraints – amongst other things he was here to show the power of intention on measurable physical feats of strength, beyond 'normal' age boundaries too.

HONOURING DEFENCES

When our Resistance is so deeply buried, we may as well not push ourselves. It is as if the ground that covers that deeply-buried Resistance has not been loosened enough yet, and the treasure of full awareness may be too hard to access without several 'broken shovels'. In this case, there is an innate wisdom in absenteeism, an unconscious knowing of the futility of unnecessary effort. 'To everything there is a season.'   Ecclesiastes 3:1-8

This is what is meant by the 'A Course in Miracles' quote at the beginning of this chapter – 'Healing is always certain.' And also from the Introduction: The 'curriculum is established... Only the time you take it is voluntary.' The strong need for safety and control is what is behind our defences. This needs to be honoured, and accepted – and in this honouring, we can expand into a different way of being, when we are ready.

OF BOUNDARIES, and SAYING 'NO'

Resistance is not a 'mistake' that we make, or even an 'error' - it is too well developed by our inner psyche. It is a means we have for creating safe boundaries, to make sure we don't 'go too far'.

If you have been a 'yes' person and a 'people pleaser' as a way of getting our needs met, perhaps it is time to try being a 'no' person for a while. The 'Oughts Musts and Shoulds', need to be re-assessed.

How important is the action that you are about to make, in the 'Grand Scheme of Things'? Are you denying our own needs in order to perform this task? Perhaps you can find a balance, a compromise, whereby the task can be performed but later, or in a simpler manner. It may be too threatening to an otherwise stable relationship, to make too many changes too quickly.

Equally, some people are stubbornly 'no' people! Almost like Resistance for Resistance' sake, as a habit – as a way of keeping power, when they otherwise feel powerless.

In that case, it may be time to say 'Yes!' – to Life!

THE POWER OF WORDS, and 'CANCELLING' NEGATIVITY

As we travel down this road of consciousness, we become increasingly aware of the power of words, and their effect in our lives, and the lives of those around us. We can even become over-concerned about that, and encounter 'sticky' patches, where we may find ourselves having thoughts (which are, after all, a selection of words unless they are pre-verbal) that are noticeably judgemental or fearful. It is easy at such times to tighten up, to Resist these thoughts about someone or oneself, trying to avoid negativity. However, in doing so, we may be setting up a suppression/denial pattern which pushes fear underground (what you Resist persists).

A suggestion at such times, is to simply acknowledge the thought, and to follow the judgemental statement in our mind with the word 'Cancel.' This has the effect of dissolving the sticky energy, and allowing a flow of more positive thoughts. To 'cancel' contracting thoughts, gives space for expansive thoughts. The book 'Your Word is Your Wand' by Florence Scovel-Shinn, is a powerful testament to the power of words.

OF PHYSICAL HEALING

All the scenarios described here are applicable to any kind of healing. However, maybe physical healing has an extra component. When energy has so coagulated that it has set up physical blockages of whatever sort, we have a problem – and we also have a solution at the same time. Since the problem is now obvious – from the acute neck pain, all the way to cancer – it then becomes easier to direct our focus. Sometimes, until it has become physical, a blockage may be too elusive to identify. When it has a 'name' (a diagnosis), a Resistance to overcome, the challenge may spur us along when we might not otherwise have bothered. It is then a **'wake-up call**,' which we can choose to attend to, beyond the physical alone.

Even though the pain (Resistance) may seem too much to bear when we are also searching for the thinking / feeling that has set it in motion, sometimes it can be an enormous motivating factor in our search for wholeness.

Chapter 13 – Rebirthing, Breathwork and Resistance

On: Being Born, and Relationships
Toxins and Metaphysics

'Love brings up anything unlike itself, for healing and release'
Always look for the HIGHEST THOUGHT in everything
Sondra Ray

BIRTH

The first experience we have of Breath is the First Breath we inhale at birth. It has been either re-experienced or somehow recorded, that this first breath is searingly hot as the air rushes into the raw and naked lungs. As a reminder, the lungs have for the first 9 months of intra-uterine life, been immersed in amniotic fluid at body temperature. This precious fluid has cushioned and nourished the foetus, and suddenly through the massaging action of being birthed, this fluid is expelled, and the now-collapsed lungs have to expand with the air pressure from the outside.

This may be the first experience of Resistance that we can have in our bodies as we are now separated from our protective womb: it is the process of withstanding this first and painful change.

Since the breath is the most fundamental basis of Life, our relationship with life itself will be interrelated with that first inhale experience. If the association with breathing itself is of an intense pain, we are very likely indeed to avoid full breathing, possibly developing asthma a little later. If its presentation is softer, cushioned by a gentle and intentional birth, there will be so much less fear of living life to the full, and appreciating the gifts of life.

Not only is the relationship to life determined by that first breath, but all our relationships will be affected by this first welcome into the world. If struggle was our experience of this first change, then we may stubbornly Resist change in the future.

Since there is so much material on this subject matter, I would prefer to refer readers to any of the books by Sondra Ray on this subject, especially Birth and Relationships (Ray & Mandel). My purpose here is to summarise from thoughts, experiences and witnessed awakenings on the subject.

What is 'Negative' in the context of carrying negative thoughts? 'Negative' is 'characterized by or displaying negation, or denial or opposition or Resistance; having no positive features' (according to the Wordweb thesaurus). We may deny our deepest fears, or reject our healing journey, but this is likely to guarantee more struggle in our lives than absolutely necessary.

EMOTIONS, STRESS and HEALTH

It may now be starting to become obvious how our emotions affect our physical health. Another and more common term for this is STRESS. How does stress occur? Stress occurs when, having been driven by our ambitions and strong desires or by our fear of not having 'enough', or even by our inability to handle (receive) 'too much', we find we have insufficient energy to sustain the drive. We struggle to maintain the impetus, but the Resistance to the inner and outer obstacles in our way, slows down our progress and creates stress, while leaving us far less able to manifest our dreams.

Now imagine that if we hold our breath in fear or terror – small panting breaths in and out – those natural toxins are not fully released, but remain in the body. Some toxins are made by neuro-transmitter breakdown, or adrenalisation with no activity. Where do these toxins go? They are stored In the liver, kidneys, heart, lungs, joints, muscles, etc, where they build up until the body can no longer prevent or Resist dis-ease or sickness from establishing itself. This could be called Emotion Sickness. Louise Hay has championed a study of insights into Metaphysical causations of illness. They are a brilliant foundation for exploring why we get ill, through the thoughts and fears we carry, usually from a long time ago.

BREATH EXCHANGE

Returning to an earlier question: what is it that we are giving back, after receiving pure energy with each breath? When we do breathe fully – not necessarily big breaths, but using the whole upper chest as well as the abdomen – we also let go on the exhale. And then all that is released is cellular toxins that have been broken down to CO_2 and some urea in the water vapour of the breath.

So in a way we are only giving back to our Planet some of our fears and anxieties. It is said that the Earth as Gaia processes any form of energy, so we can give all our pain to 'her', it will not add to the destruction of the Planet. That destruction is a result of unconscious action. This 'letting go' is an act of consciousness-raising, and as such is welcomed at a Core-level.

THE INNER MULE

During a Breathwork session - involving talking about and exploring the issues, then doing about 1 hour of Conscious Connected Breathing - is where a person's Resistances show most clearly. But if there is no permission to touch on those closed regions, they have to be respected and trusted in their timing.

The 'inner Mule' would definitely be encountered if one were to push, and try to force a change that may well be obvious to an outsider, but we have no idea how that person has travelled to get where they are today.

LIFE-ISSUES FOR HEALING (adapted from Leonard Orr's observations in the late 1970's - the 'father' of the Rebirthing movement)

The 8 'Biggies' that we all carry:-

1. Conception Trauma – the sense of separation from God at conception
2. Birth, pre-Birth (Loss of twin and/or umbilicus, difficult pregnancy), Primal Guilt and Relationships – see above
3. Infancy and School Trauma – relationships at school, as we venture out
4. Sibling Rivalry – jealousy from or towards a sibling, and effects on behaviour
5. PDS – Parental Disapproval Syndrome – trying to get attention as love or disapproval from authority figures
6. The Unconscious Death Urge – as fear of death, or desire to rejoin a loved one, we reduce our life urge and die slowly from a young age
7. Past Lives – whether we believe this as a personal truth or not, strong associations from historical events can cloud this life profoundly
8. Ancestral guilt and secrets – we can carry guilt from 7 generations back, but in healing that ancient wound, it is said we heal 7 generations into the future

RELATIONSHIPS and AREAS OF RESISTANCE TO CHANGE

Here we see those relationships with the aspects of our lives that are affected in an overall sense by the issues above, but are less fun-damental in themselves. They are the means we use to express our deepest patterns of Resistance to harmony:

Money	The presence or absence of abundance and prosperity thinking
Sex	Ease of sexual expression, in a balanced way
Addictions	We can be addicted to almost anything, if we feel a compulsion to do it
Health	By means of the 'molecules of emotion' (Pert), the neurotransmitters
Intimacy	A healthy attitude to closeness and disclosure to others
'God', Divinity	Our connection with 'things invisible' that appear to know us better than we know ourselves

SPIRITUALITY

In a way, our relationship with God / Great Spirit / Oneness / Source / the Universe can initially be a reflection of our relationship with our physical father or mother, depending on which parent is the more dominant, or a mixture of the two. But as we progress, that view widens and begins to grow into a 'knowing' of the vast and unfathomable qualities of the Divine. For some, that beautiful state of awareness is a gift from Life, or has been the result of hard work and deep contemplation.

If we are very fortunate, we get to spend time in the presence of a living Master (male or female) – those rare people who have pure intention for good, and are working to demonstrate the love and power of the Creator to as many people as will hear, and who have evolved to, and maybe even beyond Enlightenment. Being in their presence seems to plug us in relatively effortlessly, to that knowing state in ourselves, and the whole atmosphere is rarefied. It is as if we remember not to forget to remember who we are – Divine beings ourselves, a child of God "no less than the trees and stars" (Desiderata) and that each breath is a gift. We are reminded of our true essence, and we hunger and thirst to stay in that safe and beautiful place – much like an outside-inside 'womb-with-a-view'.

But then, being human, Resistance reappears as we return to our day to day lives and carry on as before, maybe slightly more 'in tune' than before. It is said, "Before enlightenment, chop wood, and carry water. After enlightenment, chop wood and carry water."

The Resistance in this case is that, on some level, we are unwilling or not really ready to grasp our divinity permanently. This is why we need reminding regularly. How frail is the human condition! And yet the thirst, the longing for that knowing state, is in itself such a sweet experience, that it also satisfies the heart abundantly.

RESULTS OF CONSCIOUS CONNECTED BREATHING

When you take courage and breathe into your fears, supported by someone who has also done this work, you begin to break down the Resistance to accepting who you truly are. All of us are deeply magnificent radiant beings at our core.

So when you allow those feelings of grief, sadness, anger, and hurt to surface and undergo transformation, you experience a profound sense of relief. You become aware that a noticeable 'chunk' of bound energy has permanently left the body – that it has left the cells of the body, where they would otherwise have remained to fester and create sickness.

Even though Breathwork is arguably the most profound of psycho-therapies simply because it is physiological as well as mending the psyche, any form of conscious and honest exploration of the self begins to invoke Self-Responsibility.

In the world of Breathwork, the premise that we are ALL 100% responsible for every aspect of our lives, is accepted. This means we cannot continue to blame others for our misfortune – it also means that we can take charge of our lives, and make huge changes consciously.

This is surprisingly not in conflict with a belief in or experience of God. It has been said that God is the creative force that always says 'YES' to everything we insist on.

Which means that, if you believe you are unworthy of happiness, God says 'yes' and strengthens that belief by 'sending along' people who reflect that same belief - people who reinforce it by agreeing with you. Conversely, if you believe you deserve love in abundance, then that is what you will receive.

If all you see around you is pain, Resistance and restraint, then that is the world reflecting how you see and believe yourself to be. If you feel a deep sense of trust and faith in life's support of your real needs, then that is what you will manifest in your life.

Once you are able to receive that support from the world and the people around, you in effect have an energy 'account' that has excess, and you can begin to give out to others who have been unable to arrive at this place yet.

In effect you can then 'pass it on'.

Chapter 14 – Resistance and Destiny

Of: Resistance to High Places;
Resistance and the Soul Path;
Quantum Connections

"Everything is determined, the beginning as well as the end, by forces over which
we have no control. It is determined for insects as well as for the stars. Human
beings, vegetables, or cosmic dust, we all dance to a mysterious tune, intoned in
the distance by an invisible piper.'   Albert Einstein
'This is a course in miracles. It is a required course. Only the time you take it is
voluntary. Free Will does not mean that you can establish the curriculum. It
means only that you can elect what you want to take at a given time. The course
does not aim to teach the meaning of love, for that is beyond what can be taught.
It does aim, however at removing the blocks to the awareness of love's
presence, which is your natural inheritance. The opposite of love is fear, but what
is all-encompassing can have no opposite. This course can therefore be summed
up very simply in this way:
Nothing real can be threatened. Nothing unreal exists.
Herein lies the peace of God'
Introduction to A Course in Miracles

DESTINY, FATE and LUCK

Destiny, Fate and Luck are often confused, and have been over time. 'Fate'
and 'Luck' have an inevitability about them, whereby one can Resist one's fate until
it stands boldly in one's path, demanding to be followed. Luck simply arrives if one
is lucky. But Destiny is deeper rooted, as if the conscious choice was made a long
time ago and was made as a Soul Contract.

Destiny represents the strength of our gifts that needs to be expressed in
order to make our presence on Earth of value to others as well as ourselves. In
fulfilling our destiny we acknowledge our gifts and use them with joy. Because our
strength lies particularly in our gifts, we can only enjoy expressing them, when we
sooner or later surrender to all the clues and indications of these strengths. This too
is inevitable.

But inherent in 'destiny versus fate,' is an unconditional love that accepts
our human weakness and our Resistance to accepting who we really are.

In other words, following the line into the centre, it appears that we are just
repeating the same pattern, causing us distress – until we acknowledge the signs
that we are 'higher up' the spiral of life – at another turning point!

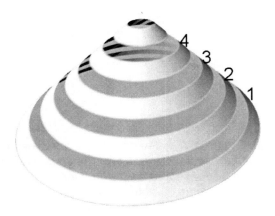

1. Point of 'entry' perhaps
2. Same pattern, different response
3. Same again only more different
4. Closer to 'Home' for E.T.!!!

Schematic Diagram to represent how we keep 'meeting' our persistent patterns along the way

RESISTING OUR OWN GREATNESS

Since who we all are, underneath however many layers we place on top, is beautiful beyond measure, we are in effect Resisting the 'high places' of ourselves.

This too has occurred within our UK Royalty – Mrs Simpson and King Edward VIII's abdication in 1936 and the reluctance of Princess Diana are recent examples. In the world of the spiritual, Krishnamurti refused to be declared the 'next World Teacher' in 1929. He felt he was not so, and he resisted this view of himself. Whether or not this Resistance was a self-limiting and self-fulfilling prophecy, we can never know. Perhaps in his deep wisdom, he realised what was called for in a Master, and accepted his own limitations, with the natural humility that was his hall-mark.

His is an example of Resistance to high places – for many people saw him as the humble Master who would never admit to his true greatness – and he spent his whole life saying to the crowds that followed him, not to look to him or anyone else for their Master.

Ironically, the very thing we crave above all else, joy in abundance, is also the very thing we Resist accepting above all else. The reasons are numerous. They can basically be summarised in this quote:

"Our deepest fear is not that we are inadequate
Our deepest fear is that we are powerful beyond measure
It is our light, not our darkness that most frightens us."
Marianne Williamson (author of 'Return to Love')
Quoted by Nelson Mandela in his Inaugural speech as President of South Africa in 1994

What would happen if you were to expand easily into your destiny? You might be the 'tall poppy' that gets its head bitten off, as you stand above the crowd. You may have the race-memory or a past-life memory of having been killed for your beliefs and principles, such as the witch-hunts for heretics. You may have to curtail your cosy life and make an effort, in the process of expressing who you truly are. But also, you may just not be ready.

So when we look at why we are bored of our lives, it may be that we are in a long-term state of Resistance to our destiny. Maybe the Resistance is not to ones' own abilities, but to those expectations from the rest of the world that accompany greatness.

Here is a diagram showing how the interplay between Resistance and 'going with the flow' can actually project us into our state of 'becoming' the greater expression of our self:

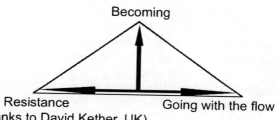

(with grateful thanks to David Kether, UK)

How much Free Will do we actually have? Can we spend a whole lifetime avoiding this issue? Yes probably. But the tree of each person's self is a certain type, and the sap within is directing its growth. No matter how much we twist and turn to move away from the challenge of bearing fruit, no matter how much it feels like being out on a limb, being that type of tree is our destiny, and we must eventually live our Soul's destination.

RESISTING ANOTHER'S GREATNESS

Sometimes our partners discover their true path before we do. Then we are faced with the need to re-evaluate the partnership. If the commitment runs deep, we have to simply adapt – this may be fraught with all kinds of friction. This friction or drag comes from the disparity between the advancing energy and that which is lagging behind. If the disparity remains for too long, it may even then threaten the relationship, if the one who has gone ahead is certain of their path. This doesn't mean that the 'Resistor' is far behind, but the gap in consciousness may become too uncomfortable to handle at that point in time.

RESISTING PLANETARY GREATNESS

Apparently this Planet, Mother Earth Gaia herself, is also undergoing a vibrational change, a sort of 'upgrade'. We are automatically part of that. Yet we do have the right to refuse to ascend with her. We do have free will to use this truly beautiful Blue Planet as our dustbin, to dishonour her people, to sully her oceans and waters. But do we truly want this?

There are many ways that can be used to slow down the evolution of the many.

How to block progress:

1. Physically: ignore the needs of future generations; disregard nature; pave the world (we *'pave paradise & put up a parking lot'* Joni Mitchell); suppress innovative inventions that don't require expensive resources;

2. Mentally: ridicule and judge people who are daring to support the raising of mass consciousness; fill the media with trivia; waste time and resources politically and financially; fill the streets and schools with chemicals, both legal and illegal, that slow down independent thought; remove art from public places; introduce computer games and TV chewing gum for the mind;
    This goes for many religions, or sub-groups of religions too

3. Emotionally: avoid all authentic communication;

4. Spiritually: cry 'cult' when something or someone new and challenging arrives to wake us up; make tradition more important than discovery of the self; make power-over more power-ful than power-with;

This cynical list is an observation of the unfortunate status quo in our world, and is something that is being fought quietly by individuals all over the world.
Thank the heavens for *grass roots.*

> *'Jack, will these changing times, motorways, power-lines,*
> *keep us apart ?*
> *well I don't think so, I saw some grass growing*
> *through the pavements today'*

The band 'Jethro Tull' – Ian Anderson and 'Jack in the Green'

It is as if the rapidly paved, covered-over parts of human consciousness are breaking out with grassy tufts, cracking the façade of control. The movement of change is so well established now at the grass-roots level, that its expressions are starting to spill over into those very institutions (as above) that are in Resistance to its progress.

People are slowly **waking up** worldwide, and we are drawing close to the *'critical mass'* needed for the chain reaction of consciousness to spread under its own momentum.

Yet until then, the darkest time is often the last hour before the dawn. Humanity seems to be polarising into 2 camps: the opponents and the proponents of the Light. It's basically **'all hands on deck' for the Light-workers.'**

This is said within the context of whether we Resist our greatness or not – apparently even the smallest part each of us can play, is of value. All of us are needed to bring about this shift.

So, could it be Mule's destiny to be a horse? Or even greater: a Centaur or a Pegasus ? Or could it be that his own peculiar characteristics developed on his journey, are enough – that the only change that really needs to happen is true love of self as it is?

CRUX OF AWARENESS

Perhaps the single most helpful and simple things we can do, when feeling overwhelmed by the darkness around us is the following thought process that was revealed to us in the new movie-
-documentary:- *'The Moses Code'*. We are reminded to look at everything around us, and say to ourselves:

I AM THAT, I AM

Meaning that 'I am everything I see, so I am not separate from anything, including the uncomfortable aspects of all I see'. This may be a way that we can energetically set up a 'Planetary Quantum Leap-Frogging,' to assist each other through to a higher consciousness.

Chapter 15 - Exercises for Working with Resistance

Of: Processes, Affirmations and Prayer
Archetypes, Astrology and Vision Quests
The Way of the Mule / the Ass
The 'sling-shot-of-change-process'

> *Take courage & accept the challenge – this is*
> *'Resistance Training' for the Soul !* CCJ
> *AWARENESS is faster than THOUGHT which is faster than LIGHT*
> *'Feel the fear and do it anyway'* (Jeffers)
> *'Man, Know Thyself'* Carved above the Delphic Oracle in Greece

As we now see, Resistance is not only everywhere, in all aspects of life, but is fundamental to the process of change. Having now seen, through all these examples of the place of Resistance in our lives, we can allow ourselves the means of working with it, rather than against it. We can even use Resistance to 'sling-shot' our evolutionary process consciously.

In the context of the topics in this book, is there an area or phrase that has caused intense disagreement? Rather than using this to simply 'feel superior' – is there a mirror at work too? The way to consciously use this disagreement is to look for key words or phrases that have stirred up an emotional response. For example, you may have some ancestral information that makes the Chapter on Political Resistance incorrect in some way – but what is the unhealed part of you that has been carried down your ancestral line in connection with that time in history?

There are so many exercises and ways of working with our Resistance that are well established. Many of you will already be using some of them. I will not list in detail the ones familiar to myself but, rather, list them in general as a reminder.

If you do not know them and wish to, and have not found enough experiential information through the internet, it may be time to check out the courses and workshops that you resonate with, from the wonderful array advertised in magazines.

THE CAN OF WORMS

It could be said that there is a choice about how to proceed. One gruesome analogy that has come to me, is an exploration of the proverbial and infamous imagery of the 'can of worms' – namely, our inner 'shadows'. We all have them. There are 3 possible choices as we consider the 'can', remembering it is chained to us, so there is no option to somehow 'eject' it. If we choose the high intention path of spiritual pursuits, without actually examining the worms, it is like opening the lid and then sitting on it, hoping the worms will never see the light of day. However, even the small amount of light that enters is enough for the worms to start to spill out, and everyone gets to see them, but slowly. And I do believe they leave the can for good once they've crawled out, if an honest intention is maintained.

Or we can choose the path of sweet ignore-ance, and drag it around everywhere with us, hoping no-one will notice it clanging and bouncing behind us. However, the worms are programmed to breed if not attended to, and the can will begin to bulge as the worms propagate. Finally they will explode, splattering debris all around us. The good news about this option is that, once exploded and cleaned up, there are a lot fewer worms remaining – however the repercussions of the collateral damage include the possibility of a lifetime's karmic clean-up.

The brave person's choice finally, is to carefully extract one worm at a time, say 'hello', examine it and 'own' it, and then let it go to have a normal worm-life. This takes time, but eventually leaves you with a beautiful 'can', with which you can be very creative – witness the million and one useful objects made in Africa out of old tin cans imaginatively recycled.

EXERCISES / PROCESSES to help:-

1. BREATHE – Get Rebirthed (Breathwork / Rebirthing / Holotropic Breathwork – the ancient Hawai'ian Kahunas understood the potency of the breath in their work, as well as the Vedic mystics; this is Air purification;
2. Pray to your Higher Power for assistance
3. Do a 'Vision Quest' with a 'Power Animal' (which does not need to be a wolf – a bunny-rabbit too has many helpful qualities) to guide and protect you; Try the deeply affirming Sweat Lodge purification;
4. Walk or lie barefoot on the grass, walk on the sand, hug a tree, walk in the rain, plant a garden – touch the earth – employ these (sometimes shamanic) methods of finding your own gentle power in a centred manner;
5. When in doubt – eat some chocolate;
6. Astrology / Human Design / Numerology / Tarot / Contemplation / Divination Cards: to highlight areas to be worked on consciously;
7. Archetypes – the collective unconscious basis of all life
    Find the one that best suits your current needs, and create a story with it – use art or music to expand on it;
8. Mirror work – looking into the mirror, saying self-esteem Affirmations: these are often badly misunderstood; most people do not like to affirm something that seems well beyond reach. They need to be adapted and personalised; and then also work with what is known as the 'response column' of reaction to this positive input.;
9. Forgiveness – perhaps a blockage stands in the way of your growth: perhaps you need to forgive someone, and of course and ultimately yourself;
10. Ancestral work, 'Family Constellations' (Hellinger) – you may be carrying a family burden, as you remain entangled in a family pattern – or you may be denying the Ancestral wisdom in your blueprint;
11. Perform Yoga or T'ai Ch'i as a slow way of accessing your inner wisdom
12. Create your own rituals supported by the 4 Elements: Earth, Air, Fire and Water - not forgetting the other 3: Below (Mother Earth)(Father Sky) – Above, and Within; Sit by the fire quietly as a Fire Purification;

13. Still in doubt ? – eat more chocolate;
14. Undertake The Journey, as developed by Brandon Bays;
15. Attend workshops run by Forum / Avatar;
16. Community Building workshops (Peck);
17. Focusing – use this body-awareness technique to assist you learning to articulate and identify areas of tension;
18. Trust who steps forward into your life synchronously now
19. Use the force-of-Resistance: feel the tension between your 'Current Reality' and what you want as your goal, like a stretched elastic ready to release and arrive at its target – as described by Robert Fritz in TFC 'Technologies for Creating'
20. Guess what? Bring out the chocolate – could be cocoa;
21. Resourcing – work with the Peter Levene focus of gently unravelling trauma;
22. If you wish to hold on to your Resistance, the 'Way of the Mule' may be the way forward for you.;
23. Working with A Course in Miracles, using a lesson a day for a year is very committed, but worth reigning in your 'Inner Mule' and sticking with it. The lessons are profound and life changing;
24. Attend a course in Non-Violent Communication (Rosenberg), to help to identify your Un-Met Needs;
25. Attend a Holotropic Breathwork (Grof) workshop – you may be in the middle of a 'Spiritual Emergence' process, if you are struggling with your new awareness;
26. Work through the Victim-Freedom Cycle (as outlined by Colin Sisson) – you may be stuck in a loop of repetition, even though you feel ready to change;
27. Employ the time-management technique of telling your mind 'I'll just do 20 connected breaths', (Ask a Breathworker to demonstrate, and take you through 10 sessions of 'Rebirthing-Breathwork, so you learn to understand this process) or 'I'll just do this focused piece of 'homework' – it gets round the Resistant mind with trickery, since before you know it, you will be continuing to do what you were Resisting – and with ease too;
28. BREATHE in the bath – as water purification, and have the bathroom gently lit with a 'tea-light' candle – that usually shifts things quickly;
29. Sometimes 'smudging' with fresh sage, or incense, helps clear the air literally;
30. MEDITATION – follow through on whichever technique or teacher attracts you, or a teaching that challenges your view of reality;
31. Watch an uplifting movie, it may inspire your transformation;
32. Take a cup of quality hot chocolate to bed, you deserve it
33. Just say 'Yes', but check in with yourself:- does it feel right? Do you resonate with what is presenting itself;

ARCHETYPES

'Archetypal' means a pattern which is universal and existent in all people in all cultures in all periods of history' (Liz Greene). For example, in every culture, birth, death, 'the fool', lovers, kings or rulers, and priests (or 'witch doctors') are found.

In the ancient study of Astrology, SATURN is seen as the archetypal great teacher who rewards the diligent, if you really address his lessons pertaining to respecting boundaries. The location of Saturn in your chart will show up the area in your make-up where the most Resistance exists. For example: Saturn in Cancer would show up issues around staying at home; Saturn in Taurus - difficulties with money etc.

Perhaps the greatest Archetypal teacher is Death – The Reaper, who makes us reap what we have sewn. Where the greatest change is occurring, that is where the death of the old, and birth of the new is brought about. As we are naturally fearful of change, our Resistance is likely to become most evident here.

SENTENCE COMPLETION as an AID

This is a very useful tool in finding out just what you are thinking below the surface. Most of us are so used to having our judgements and mental commentaries, that we are unable to find what is driving them. This is an easy way of discovering just that.

In this context, a simple self-questioning sentence, that can be modified to suit each person, is:

Q - The areas that I am aware of in my life that I know I have Resistance to, are …
Q - The subjects or phrases (in this book) that caused me to notice my areas of Resistance are:…

Complete these sentences – you may find many answers; but if you are struggling, stretch yourself to finding 10. When you have done that ask yourself:

Q – The MAIN area I have Resistance in, is …

You can create more specific Questions to narrow down the clues: Universal areas of Resistance are in health, relationships, work, money, sex and spirituality.
Then you are ready to begin working with that answer.

The first Step, like admitting to an addiction, is to acknowledge it to yourself, then to someone else. It does appear to be stronger than us at this stage. If it is very strong and a source of deep anxiety, maybe it's time to pray for help.

To make a Prayer for help, we can address any one of the increasing number of Light Beings that are gathering to help us in this testing and transitional time. If you want to 'hedge your bets', being uncertain as to whom to address in particular, try this little mnemonic of 'MAGIC':-

MASTER/S	- Ascended Masters & Saints, Living Masters (male & female)
ANGELS	- Hosts of Angels and Archangels who await our prayers and requests
GUIDES	- Our own lifelong and temporary Guides are here to help
I AM	- **I AM THAT, I AM** ('The Moses Code' film)
CREATOR	- The Unbreakable Mirror, That Which is Undeniable, Great Spirit, The Unwavering Truth, the Immeasurable, the Great Architect, The Universe, The Almighty, Highest Intelligence, The Word, God, That Which can be experienced as the Infinite within the Finite (that's us)(Search for Knowledge of the Soul's Higher Self)

Then ask for the help you need. Often there are signs that your request has been heard by an invisible Light-source, before you have articulated your sentence. The intention to reach out, with clarity for what you need, is enough to draw help.

ABRAHAM-HICKS

'Working with the Abraham-Hicks' way of understanding *'the Art of Allowing'*, we are encouraged to look at *how we* Resist what we choose consciously – what we do to keep our healing, or our needs fulfilled, from coming to us. What is the 'Vibrational Gap' between what you want, and it's arrival? They remind us that to focus on what we don't have, adds more Resistance to the vision. When others around us are the indicators of how much Resistance we are still putting up, by reflecting our inner sub-conscious state - this is a wonderful teaching tool. We can thank them for showing us what we still need to work on.

The same with disease. What chronic emotional imbalance pre-indicates the blossoming into disease? They say that every emotion, which comes from every sub-conscious thought, is due to us not keeping up with the higher aspect of ourselves that is advancing ahead of us.

In this way also, there is a 'Vibrational Gap'.

When receiving healing, the healer acts to soften our Resistance to healing ourselves. No-one can be healed if their Resistance is too high.

Some 'Abraham' sayings that are particularly relevant:-

1. *'If you don't meet Resistance with Resistance, it dissipates dramatically. It just softens. Try it!'*
2. *'Negative emotion is your indicator of Resistance, while positive emotion is your indicator of Allowance';*
3. *'Illness or pain is just an extension of negative emotion. When you are no longer feeling any Resistance to it,' it has no further need to be there';*
4. *'All of you are allowing - through the crack of least Resistance!';*
5. *'Resistance is about believing that you are vulnerable or susceptible to something not wanted;'*
6 .*'That's why so many of us teach meditation. Because when you stop thought, you stop Resistant thought';*

7 .'As you are reaching, in a determined way, for the Path of Least Resistance, anything that is Resistant within you will'... be shown up;
8. 'It's All About Vibrational Relativity';
9. 'If you were allowing Source Energy to pour through you in the abundant way that it would if you were not Resisting it,' you would manifest everything and be in perfect health;

THE 'SLING-SHOT-OF-CHANGE' PROCESS

The term *'slingshot of change'* has been coined by me, in memory of the intense challenge faced by the crew of Apollo 13 in 1970, when it was decided to 'slingshot' the ailing spacecraft around the Moon's gravitational field, in order to get it back to Earth. The 'worst-case-scenario' happened, and was dealt with in this extra-ordinary manner.

The 'best-case-scenario' for someone with huge Resistance to life, is to face the source of the fear of life, and return transformed.

To begin this process, you will need to get clear on an aspect of your life that is getting in your way, that your friends or partners, (at home or in business), tell you is a recurring theme. If you are still not sure, allow the process itself to tell you – but decide before you start to trust the answer that comes to you – it is too easy to doubt ones' intuitions.

If this seems scary because of what you might find, honour the fear, and work with someone who has a bigger picture overall, and has your highest interests at heart, whether this is a friend or your therapist.

This is a visualisation involving being in a relaxed state – you will need to be lying down or sitting as comfortably as possible. You can have calming non-vocal music going on – this can be new to you, or it can have an emotional association – either is good. You will undergo a journey in space, to an important centre in your universe.

This centre is where a major Resistance lives – you will have the courage to make the full journey to that place, and back again safely. You may invite a known or unknown role model to accompany you, to give you further courage, or simply to share your experience.

The Visualisation

Imagine you are able to fly like an eagle.

Enjoy the sights, sounds and sensations of this amazing ability. Feel your well-oiled feathers untouched by cold or severe weather. Feel the ease of flight, as you need only flap your giant wings once or twice, rising higher and higher on the air streams. As you spiral upwards, an unexpected force lifts you with greater ease, and you enter the Earth's atmosphere, unaffected by the lack of oxygen. You look below you at your fast-receding home. You marvel at its beauty, its colours, its' natural radiance.

As your Sky-walking trajectory takes you further into space, with Earth becoming a distant blue-green ball, you realise that not only can you breathe here, but you are breathing better than you normally do. You feel free and un-inhibited by society, by your family, by yourself. You might even want to dance out here in space – feeling weightless floating upwards in an ocean of dark-matter to envelop you and carry you.

As you head out past our neighbouring planets you are particularly enthralled by Saturn and 'his' rings of particulate matter, humming through his own orbit – this is the Lord of Time.

As you leave our solar system, your light and your time speeds up – travel is faster and easier. As you traverse the universe, you become aware of an absence of light somewhere in the rapidly approaching distance. You realise this is a Black Hole.

But you have no fear, because it is your very own Black Hole that you created somewhere back in time. It is no ordinary Black Hole, however, as it is the outward manifestation of a major area of Resistance you have in your life. Not only that, but its gravitational pull is incomplete. It draws you painlessly but inexorably only to its edge. Your 'retro-boosters' work well, as you slow to a speed that allows you to come to rest at its edge - you can now perch on its 'event-horizon'. It is as if you are able to lie face down on a platform overhanging a deep, dark pool swirling silently beneath you.

As you look into this pool of awareness, shapes and figures become increasingly clear. They form into people and places that hold memory for you. They are here to help you understand your Resistance since they live here in this 'Black Hole'.

They are the Higher aspects, the Souls of their original selves, and wish to honour and aid you. Now you may ask them for signs and symbols that will help you understand this named Resistance.

If you are a 'visual' type, let the images build the picture or remind you of a past scene that holds a key.

If you are an 'auditory' type, let the messages come clearly to you as comprehensible clues or memories of spoken or overheard phrases. There may be only one phrase or word but trust it, especially if it repeats itself.

If you are a 'kinaesthetic' type, let yourself feel what is being conveyed. There may be a painful memory connected with touch, which has built up your Resistance to touch.

When you feel you have received enough information, one of the participants in this scene steps forward to give you a precious gift. The gift is a symbol of this awareness, which you can take home with you as a reminder. What is it? Another aspect of this gift is that it also helps you integrate this experience during your journey home, and beyond. You thank them for drawing you out here into this vast dark and surprisingly warm space.

As the scene fades, you become fully aware again of where you are. To your initial dismay, you feel a sort of rumbling beneath you – the Black Hole is getting smaller, it is shrinking in front of your eyes, and becoming more and more dense. It becomes so small you can barely see it, and there is a sense of impending sudden change as it swallows some of the space around it. It is spinning faster into itself, and you are spinning with it, round and round. If this makes you feel sea sick, imagine you are able to only see the times when you arrive back at that place you were resting on.

And then it stops.

Suddenly it explodes silently in slow motion, spitting out beautiful new stars in every direction. The force of this sudden expansion pushes you, and you move rapidly back the way you came

As you recognise our solar system again, you relax and trust the process of return. You enter the Earth's atmosphere, easily finding your wings again, resting on the thermals as they bring you gently back to the ground.

You look down at your hands – you have a gift that has come from the most unlikely place – the Black Hole of your Resistance. Since you have dared to undergo this courageous journey, space will never be the same – your presence and observation of the truth captured by the Black Hole has exploded it, and created new galaxies already.

The exhale of your Black Hole that has occurred since you had the courage to look into it, has spun you round like a 'sling-shot', and returned you to your home, but as a changed person. At this stage, the change may only be in the form of understanding. You can choose to keep your Resistance – but consciously this time, until you are ready to let it go. It is a now a true point of choice.

Or you can allow the change, and let go of the Resistance right now. The feeling of needing this obstruction is simply an illusion – it has been a coping mechanism, for dealing with your old fears. You are now aware that it no longer serves you. It can die. And you can thank it for having protected and served you all this time.

'When you have learned to accept the past & you have made peace with it, it will leave you in peace.' Moshe Feldenkrais

BLIND SPOTS

Everyone has 'Blind Spots'. They may even be hidden from our nearest and dearest, being so deeply interwoven with our personalities and our mannerisms. If we ever discover what they are, we find them to be quite shocking, as they are large and integrated into important areas of our lives. If anyone else does recognise this 'weak area' there is an unspoken drive not to tell, because you can be sure it is not a welcome observation. It is an area of weakness, because it runs our lives quietly in the background, affecting all our important decisions. It doesn't seem to matter how much we genuinely want to be conscious on our daily and inner journeys, by it's very nature, it is unseen. Every time we turn around to look at it or for it, it 'travels' with us, and we never see it.

I am not aware of a way of finding Blind Spots. This can be the source of our deepest Resistance, the last bastion of our defences. If we truly wish to find it, our only hope at least for some, may be to hold out for a Divine Cavalry, or an attack from apparent enemies and from an unexpected angle – a 'Custer's Last Stand' of the ego. Perhaps there is a way of integrating this defensive regiment (to continue the battle analogy); a way of incorporating the feisty minions. Perhaps a little village of compassionate workers and laughing monks can melt their hearts slowly over time. Or perhaps the most compassionate thing to do (in the long run) would be to destroy it.

This is the action of our Soul Mate, the true one who says or does something that so rocks our world, that topples our towers, that there is no time for the defences to gather. We can only fall. And the further we fall, the higher we seem to rise later in time. This is truly the action of someone who loves us so much, they have agreed at a Soul level to be the apparent enemy, to get inside our most intricate defences, and then perform this heinous act, that ultimately may even appear to destroy us.

But whenever the final recovery occurs, we are raised so much higher than we were at the start, that we may end up being 'higher' energetically than the 'perpetrator'.

So our Blind Spot is the weakest spot, but it also holds the potential for the most profound healing and advancement of our Soul's evolution. For this awakening, we can only pray for someone – yes another hu-man being, who may also be 'God-in-action' – to have the courage to do this for us. This potential makes our Blind Spot the *'Pièce de Résistance.'*

EXPLORING the 'UPSIDE' of RESISTANCE

Something we can do is to take some of the themes from chapters in this book, and use them as a way to determine where our Resistance lies, and why it is there. What are we protecting? What are we *successfully* protecting? Why does it need protecting? What needs to show up before we feel ready to allow it to change? The 'success' is the 'Upside'. When considering that we have Resistance to life, or any aspect of life, it is very easy to feel that an unpleasant facet of ourselves, something we'd rather keep hidden, has been exposed. But seen as a coping and protective mechanism, we can congratulate ourselves on creatively finding ways to survive, and to buy time, until we are ready to upgrade.

Then we can begin.

Taking themes from some of the chapters in this book, we can explore our relationship with them. For example, where do you stand relative to the authority of the State, or your religious organisation, or even to God ? What is your attitude to your physical health, how do you take care of yourself ? Do you take life too seriously, in a way Resisting seeing the humour in everyday life? Do you allow yourself creative expression, through the arts, music, theatre? Or does your fear of failure stop the fullness of your honest expression ? Have you somehow missed out on your adolescent rebellion, trying to please your parents? Has a difficult birth, or childhood difficulty set up a fear of all transitions and change, so that you resist life itself, as it attempts to love you? Are you reluctant to ask for help on your healing journey?

A simple summary of the process, and its more evident 'upside' is this:– fear / hopelessness / frustration / breakthrough / sense of achievement. It is worth the 'squirming' for the result !

It is time to feel gratitude for your Resistance to date, and then to move on. It has taken care of you, yet if left as it is, you will not progress, you will not evolve. Resistance is the ego in action, the 'status quo' that keeps us in our comfort zones. Surrender to the flow of life, to our 'higher self, our 'higher power', is the challenge and the delight. Exploring your Resistance brings to you the 'Upside'. These are the benefits that come from the clues highlighted by your honest awareness. That's how it works. There is the value.

Chapter 16: Resistance to Surrender of the Ego

Of: Death of the ego
Remembering the Divine Self and our Purpose
Soul Path and Soul Contracts

Resistance is what surfaces in the company of Enlightenment   CCJ
*'The struggle is between one part that wants to sleep, and
the other part that wants to wake up'
(like 2 fists pushing against each other)*   Prem Rawat
*'Surrender and Resistance are coupled energies. In linear terms, Resistance is
first, surrender follows, and ultimately the two
precipitate ecstasy'*
Chris Griscom, (p.5) in her book *'Ecstasy is a new Frequency'*
*Ego exists through Resistance.
This has to be understood very deeply.
The more you fight, the more 'you' will be there.*   Osho
*Laughter takes place when the soul tricks the mind
'Gurus are here not to tech us about their divinity, but to
teach us about our own'*   Oprah Winfrey
'E-go, E-going, E-gone'   *'Swami Beyondananda'*
'The Swami's 'electric' cure for Resistance is the mantra 'Ooohhmm'

Ultimately all Resistance comes down to Resisting the process of surrendering the ego. Even this sentence will cause great discomfort, and probably much reaction, and yet it feels true. What else is there now?

The fear coming from this enlightened transformation may be based on a belief that your ego will 'go' all at once, and leave you in a state of non-existence – that you will die. This is a biologic and ego function based solely on physical survival. However the reality is so different. Once you begin to discover the insidious nature of the ego, you begin to desire to reach past its whining, childish, smart, cunning, devious, and frankly cruel and manipulative ways. For this to be possible, we need the presence in our lives of a (much) higher Being or Master. It is as if the surrender, the 'Ok I give up, don't shoot me' white flag of admission of weakness, has to be given to someone who knows what to do with it.

At this point, the journey has truly begun; and it is a journey.

The SOUL PATH and SOUL CONTRACTS

We all tend to Resist our spiritual journey, or, if we don't resist the actual journey, then we resist part of it at times.

It is understood by many, that the purpose of our life is to find our way back to the Father-Mother (the Divine), to complete the circle of 'leaving home', and like the Prodigal Son, be welcomed and celebrated for returning Home. I believe that this is everyone's purpose in life – and in addition, to learn to enjoy our Selves along the way. We also seek to find our more personal (soul) purpose in our lives.

Why are we here having these particular experiences? What can we contribute? It's as if our general Purpose is to be given to us by the Creator, through all the gifts of being alive. And so, it seems that our personal purpose is to give back to the Creator through using our gifts, to 'bless' others as well as ourselves.

Why do we Resist the journey?

Because it hurts at times, or because we are lazy by nature, even if in every other respect we are hardworking. For some, inner discomfort is actually the hardest to bear, and there can be a tendency to want to wriggle out of uncomfortable feelings. Being aware of our Resistance can be helpful to motivate us to work through these discomforts to emerge.

But it's these very feelings that indicate the beginning of the emergence of the butterfly from the pupa. It has been observed that if one tries to aid a butterfly by peeling back the pupa so it can emerge, it will die – it actually needs the Resistance of the cocoon to break through and emerge strong.

When you begin our journey into consciousness, you often attract new people who either encourage and support you, or people who remind you of the comfort of ignorance, the 'devil you know'. These people are manifesting your own inner Resistance and are there to show you where in particular you are reluctant to move on – they are being wonderful reflectors!

You need all the help you can get to let go of past hurts, and to let go of negative attachments. Help to purge, cleanse, and detoxify your body and mind. And what will you find underneath? Something that was there all the time - the beautiful, the translucent, the luminescent Self - that spark of the Divine that you have always been. And what have you created along the way, in order to avoid seeing that beauty?

What haven't you? If Thought is Creative, where you are the thinker that thought something negative about yourself – then you are also the thinker that can think something positive about the very same aspect of your life (Ray)

BEYOND the EGO-CHILD

the best things in life
have fleas

The ego is like a child, needy for attention of any sort, through any means, willing to wreck any process with its whining and its snide comments. This is where the 'Resistor' resides. Yet acknowledging the 'child', by saying 'thank you for sharing, but I will continue to do this that I know benefits me' allows the ego to 'feel heard', yet reminding it of who is the adult, whose process allows the whole family to have their needs met.

Simon Drew – www.simondrew.co.uk

In my ideally humble opinion, the drive for the ego to be 'right', is probably second only to the drive for survival Of course this could be my own ego speaking, and in that case I must be right!

"*It is possible to travel to the source of Resistance to uncover its underlying purpose and dissolve it with the powerful healing instruments of truth and compassion.*

Resistance is a survival mechanism of the emotional body. It is produced through the biochemistry of fear.

We resist that which we fear because of our association of experience – experience which includes a vast repertoire of what we call time and space.'

'The emotional body uses Resistance as a technique for controlling experience.

Resistance helps us stay within the territory of our emotional-body themes. The ego identifies itself through our experiences and never truly desires to let go of them, even if they are negative (and) self-identification is crucial to the ego's survival ...

(But) the ego can be released from the bonds of fear.

How? Through states of wonderment and ecstasy...

Then we can begin viewing the hologram of the multi-dimensional self. The expansion of the consciousness to embrace that multi-dimensional reality is what enlightenment is all about.'

Chris Griscom

(The reason for including this long quote is that there is so much richness in its perspective – so much so that it would be incomplete, quoted only in part.)

So now, having started on the conscious journey, you may see your life as a glass of water that has appeared clear, but has a thick deposit of mud on the bottom (see Chapter 10 on Teenagers). As the purity coming from the input of Light stirs up the water it is pouring into, the mud there is stirred up too. Remember it is on its way out, so carry on pouring in that Light, as it is the only way the water will become fully clear.

Before and approaching Enlightenment, you battle with the ego, especially as you get more conscious of its subtle manipulations. However, it can also be more 'sneaky', and you can find yourself with a 'spiritual ego', that will be harder to work on consciously, because the mind becomes more sophisticated. This may then presage a harder 'fall' – all for the purpose of healing and evolution, of course.

BOW TO THE SOURCE

You may know all there is to know ABOUT the 'world beyond' – you may be able to quote all the 'great minds' in the field, and even actually and authentically understand Quantum Physics and the Chaos Theory (and what they are attempting to explain) – but until you turn round and face yourself and 'slay the dragon', it is only a broad version of 3D - Matrix thinking.

Ultimately no-one can fail – you will all succeed in the return Home, and have an amazing journey on the way. The voyage is the goal, since it is often said we never 'arrive' – so we might as well enjoy the ride.

The answer is, when in doubt, bow to the Source and the Force, which has no ego. 'It' knows when you are ready, when it can go straight into the centre of your Resistance past all the dumb-founded battalions of your stronghold, the Fort of Reason. Then you can come out with your hands in the air, uncovering your heart, saying 'I Surrender'. That is when you discover that what you were

Resisting all this time was your best friend. You won't believe it before that moment.

The POWER OF NOW (Eckhart Tolle)

Once again the full quotes are needed here.

(Tolle – pp156 & 181) 'If there is a conflict between an emotion and a thought, the thought will be the lie and the emotion will be the truth. Not the ultimate truth of who you are, but the relative truth of your state of mind at that time (since emotion is the body's reaction to the mind) … All inner Resistance (my capital 'R' in order to highlight, as usual through this book – CJ) is experienced as negativity in one form or another. All negativity is Resistance …

'As there are no problems in the Now, there is no illness either. If you have a major illness, use it for enlightenment. Withdraw 'Time' from the illness – no past or future…. When your pain is deep, all talk of surrender will probably seem futile and meaningless anyway. When your pain is deep, you will likely have a strong urge to escape from it, rather than surrender to it. You don't want to feel what you feel. There is no escape, no way out. There are many pseudo-escapes – work, drink, drugs, anger, projection, suppression and so on – but they don't free you from the pain. Suffering does not diminish intensity when you make it unconscious. When you deny emotional pain, everything you do or think as well as your relationships, become contaminated with it.

'When there is no way out, there is always a way through. Face it, feel it fully, give all your attention to the feeling, not to the person or the event or the situation that seems to have caused it. Since it is impossible to get away from the feeling, the only possibility of change is to move into it: otherwise nothing will 'shift'. So give your complete attention to what you feel, keep feeling the grief, fear, dread, loneliness, whatever it is. Stay alert, stay present – present with your whole being. Being with every cell in your body. As you do so, you are bringing a light into this darkness. This is the flame of your consciousness. At this stage you don't need to be concerned with surrender any more. It has happened already.

How? Full attention is full acceptance, is surrender.

By giving full attention you use the Power of the Now. No hidden pocket of Resistance can survive it. Presence removes Time – without Time, no suffering, no negativity can survive.

Since Resistance is inseparable from the mind, relinquishment of Resistance – surrender – is the end of the mind as your master, the imposter pretending to be 'you', the false god. All judgement and all negativity dissolve. The Realm of Being, which had been obscured by the mind, then opens up. Suddenly a great stillness arises within you, and an unfathomable sense of peace, there is great joy. And within that joy is love. And at the innermost core, there is the sacred, the immeasurable, that which cannot be named. I don't call it finding God … God is Being itself. Not a being. There can be no subject-object relationship here, no duality, no 'you and God'.

Choice implies consciousness…without it, you have no choice .. this means that you are compelled to think, feel and act in certain ways according to the conditioning of your mind (the devil you know). Present-moment awareness creates a GAP not only in the stream of mind, but also in the past-future continuum. Nothing truly new and creative can come into this world except through that gap, that clear space of infinite possibility.

'It always looks as if people have a choice, but that is an illusion. As long as your mind, with its conditioned patterns runs your life, as long as you are your mind, what choice do you have? None. You are not even there. The mind-identified state is severely dysfunctional. It is a form of insanity. Almost everyone is suffering from this illness in varying degrees. The moment you realise this, there can be no more resentment. How can you resent someone's illness? The only appropriate response is compassion … and forgiveness is unnecessary (realising that nothing could ever touch the radiant essence of who you are).

Here is a comparison of vibrations of different states of being, when thinking either from the Unlimited Spirit Mind or the Limited Ego Mind (from the Loving Relationships Training LRT, as devised by Sondra Ray in the 1980's):-

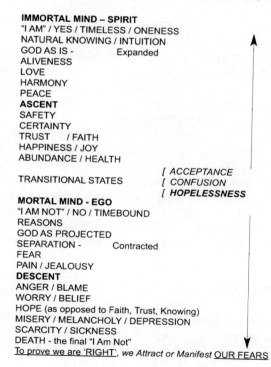

IMMORTAL MIND – SPIRIT
"I AM" / YES / TIMELESS / ONENESS
NATURAL KNOWING / INTUITION
GOD AS IS -   Expanded
ALIVENESS
LOVE
HARMONY
PEACE
ASCENT
SAFETY
CERTAINTY
TRUST   / FAITH
HAPPINESS / JOY
ABUNDANCE / HEALTH

TRANSITIONAL STATES   [ACCEPTANCE
                             [CONFUSION
                             [*HOPELESSNESS*

MORTAL MIND - EGO
"I AM NOT" / NO / TIMEBOUND
REASONS
GOD AS PROJECTED
SEPARATION -   Contracted
FEAR
PAIN / JEALOUSY
DESCENT
ANGER / BLAME
WORRY / BELIEF
HOPE (as opposed to Faith, Trust, Knowing)
MISERY / MELANCHOLY / DEPRESSION
SCARCITY / SICKNESS
DEATH - the final "I Am Not"
To prove we are 'RIGHT', we Attract or Manifest <u>OUR FEARS</u>

It is said that 'confusion' is a very high state (Ray): it is one of the feelings at the junction between unconsciousness, and consciousness, so it heralds great change. Confusion can also be the judgement you have about the Resistance you express, as you make that further transition. It's hard to take those final steps of such a huge change. It's like you are stepping out of an old skin that doesn't fit any more, but the new skin hasn't yet grown fully, so you are in a 'no-man's-land' of neither state being comfortable (Artemis). And what happens is that situations arise or people make comments, that either plunge you further into confusion, because they reflect your uncertainty, or they reflect your Resistance, giving you permission to revert to the older and easier way of being. But this is so unsatisfying once you have started to really choose conscious living. Sooner or later those old choices lose their appeal.

MAKING A DIFFERENCE

When my ego has taken a battering, and my self-esteem is low, and I can't quite find my place in the world, or in my own heart, I look at where I have made a difference to other people. Where have you made a difference as you've gone through the gift of your life ? Where have you reminded people of who they really are ? It may only be one person (very unlikely to be only one) whose world would be the poorer without your input at any point in time. Be proud of and grateful to yourself - you deserve it. And there's always more to give and to receive.

CONSCIOUS RESISTANCE

There is a point to all of this. That is, to make the Resistance conscious: to 'name the beast'. That begins to loosen it and take its power away, so that when you are ready to let it go, which could even be in many years' time, it may then just fall away with very little pain, struggle or fear. It is there now for a reason - trust that. Trust the process and be willing to be honest with yourself.

At times like this, it will be necessary to choose courageously. Perhaps if the Resistance is too deeply rooted, it may be necessary to look as closely as you can, while leaving it in place, much like a weed in the garden. But the process of daring to look, is like applying weed-killer (organic, of course), and then digging around the offending weed, thus exposing its roots to sunlight. Sooner or later it will not be able to sustain itself, and will fall away.

It's OK – have compassion for yourself. Weeds are beautiful too. Weeds are nature's way of filling gaps with colour and nourishment. And they're often much more obviously 'unique'!

RESOLUTION of RESISTANCE

Like all things in motion in our 3D universe, Resistance will always resolve itself. Like discordant music, harmony has to result. In chaos, order and rest come to pass. Inertia must change, because of all the external effects on an object that is still or is constantly moving – something will stop it or start it and cause it to change – it is inevitable. Unbending Resistant materials may break under pressure – but even that will, in time, resolve when nature takes over and heals, and closes, and uses the resultant raw materials in new creative ways. Resistant touch will resolve itself into a fall, sooner or later, - how else are we to learn? Even Resistance itself is subject to entropy (break-down) in the presence of the heat of the moment. And Light resolves itself when it lands on the eye of the beholder.

Equally, Resistance within the individual's psyche will always and ultimately resolve itself. The timing for that may not be visible to many observing the life of that person. Even apparent tragedy or failure is success in process, in a much larger picture.

The purpose of this study is to encourage us all to allow the Resistance. It has its place, its reasons and its seasons, so make a conscious choice to allow it for now, until you are ready to let go. Meanwhile, practice the art of recognising when you're ready, and allow Life to lead you to your next chapter, with the 'help' that arrives in the most unexpected disguises.

Well, Mule is now stubbornly 'on the path' and nothing will stop him – he has crossed to the other side of the fence to the sweet sweet grass of Home, munching contentedly on the Elyssian Fields of inner freedom.

And remember, even when you've 'fallen on your Ass', you can still enjoy the ride – you are being carried at such times !

<u>Synonyms for Resistance</u>

Chapters
All Active, except * (a passive form of Resistance)

Antagonise	Sports	7
Avoidance	Change	11
Blockage	Medicine	6
Challenging	Science	3 and 10
Contraction	Medicine	6 and 2 (Black Holes)
Defended	Change	11
Disobedient	Politics	5 and 10
Drag	Science	2 and 14
Fight	Political	5 and 14
Friction	Science	2 and 14
*Inertia	Science	3
Inflexibility	Architecture	9 and 11
Inhibition	Change	15
Laziness	Word	1
Objection	Politics	5
Obstacle	Word	1
Obstruction	Exercises	15
Opposition	Politics	5
Prevention	Change	11
Procrastinating	Change	11
Protesting	Politics	5
Rebellious	Teenagers	10
Recalcitrant	Teenagers	10
Reducer	Electricity	2
Reluctance	Change	11
Refusal	Destiny	14
Restraint	Change	11
Rigid	Architecture	9 and 7
Stubborn	Change	11
Unyielding	Change	7 and 11
Withstand	Rebirth	7 and 12

To stand up or offer resistance to somebody or something

<u>TOPIC INDEX</u>

General Index

BIBLIOGRAPHY

'A Course in Miracles –(1975) Vol.3, *Manual for Teachers'* Foundation for Inner Peace; Channelled by Helen Schucman

Ader Robert (1990, 2nd ed.) ed.: *'Psychoneuroimmunology'*, NY Academic Press.

Becker, Suzy (1990) *'All I need to know I learned from my cat'* Workman NY

Beyondananda /Baerman Steve, (1989) "*Driving Your Own Karma',* Destiny USA

Blechschmidt, M.D. and Gasser R.F., (1978) *'Biokinetics and Biodynamics of Human Differentiation'* Charles Thomas USA

Bogart, Anne (2001) "*A Director Prepares – 7 essays on art and theatre*" Routledge London

Braden, Gregg (2008) *'The Spontaneous Healing of Belief, Shattering the Paradigm of False Limits'* Hay House

Chopra, D., (1990*) 'Quantum Healing: exploring the Frontiers of Mind-Body Medicine',* Bantam .

Chopra, Deepak, (1993) *'Ageless Body, Timeless Mind'*, Harmony-Crown, NY

Ciba Foundation Symposium (1972),*' Physiology, Emotion and Psychosomatic Illness'*

Cousins, Norman (1995 updated from 1974) *'The Anatomy of an Illness (as perceived by the patient)'* Norton.

Emoto, Masaru (2004) *'The Hidden Messages in Water'* Beyond Words Pub. OR

Gallwey, Tim (1986) *'The Inner Game of Music'* Anchor
Feldenkrais, Moshe (1985) *'The Potent Self* - A Study of Spontaneity & Compulsion'* Frog Ltd, CA

Fritz, Robert, (1985) *'The Path of Least Resistance',* DMA Inc. Salem MA

Greenberg, D.B., (1995, Mar-Apr.) book review of Damasio: 'Descartes' Error, Emotion, Reason and the Human Brain', in *Psychosomatics*, 36(2), p.151 and 152.

Gendlin, Eugene, (1982) *'Focusing – how to open up your deeper feelings and Intuition'* , Bantam Books

Grof, Stanislav and Christina, (1992) *'The Stormy Search for the Self'* Tarcher NY

Hay, Louise: (1987) *'You can heal your life'* Hay House,

Hellinger, Bert (1998) *'Love's Hidden Symmetry'* (Family Constellations) Verlag, Zeig, Tucker and Thyson Inc

Holden, Robert, (2000) *'Shift Happens',* Hodder and Stoughton

Hutchinson, Michael, (1998) *'Megabrain'* Beech Tree Books NY

Jeffers, Susan (1988) *'Feel the fear and do it anyway'* Ballantine

Jennings, Celia : (April 1998) *'Emotional Release with Osteopathic Treatment'* - New Zealand Charter Journal – Vol 1 Nos. 4 and 5

Johnson, Spencer, (1998) *'Who moved my cheese'* Random House

Kaku, Michio, (1994) *'Hyperspace: A Scientific Odyssey through Parallel Universes, Time Warps and the 10th Dimension'* OUP NY

Levene, Peter A. (1997) *'Waking the Tiger, Healing Trauma'* North Atlantic Books
McTaggart, Lynne (2001) *'The Field'* Harper-Collins, UK

Korr, Irwin, (1995, Mar.) *'Osteopathy: Taking its Rightful Place'*; address at Osteopathy 2000 Conference, London. Obtainable from Osteopathic schools.

Liberman, Jacob (1991) *'Light, Medicine of the Future'* Bear and Co.

Locke, Stephen E. and Colligan, D. (1987) *'The Healer Within,'* Mentor, Penguin.

Lowen, Alexander (1976) *Bioenergetics* , NY Penguin.

Mindell, Arnold (1995) *'Sitting in the Fire – Large Group Transformation Using Conflict and Diversity'* Portland Lao Tse Press

Myss, Caroline M – (2002) *'Sacred Contracts: Awakening Your Divine Potential'* Bantam Paperback

Myss, Caroline M (1998) *"Why People Don't Heal and How They Can'* Bantam

Ornstein, Robert ,and Swencionis,C.,(ed.)(1990) *'The Healing Brain,'* Guilford

Pearsall, Paul P. (1998) *'Heart's Code - Tapping the Wisdom and Power of Our Heart's Energy'* Salem Press,

Peck, M.Scott, (1990) *'The Different Drum – the creation of true community, the first step to world peace'.* Arrow Books

Redfield, James: (1993) *'Celestine Prophecy'*, Bantam Books

Pert, Candace, (1997) *'Molecules of Emotion – why you feel the way you feel'* Scribner NY

Ray, Sondra and Bob Mandel, (1985)*'Birth and Relationships'* Celestial Arts CA,

Rosenberg, Marshall B. Ph.D (2003) *'Nonviolent Communication: A Language of Life'* Puddle Dancer Press

Schmoll, H.J., (1992) *'Psychoneuroimmunology : interactions between brain, NS, behaviour and endocrine and immune systems,'* Hogrefe and Huber.

Scientific American, readings from, (to 1972), (with Intro. by) Richard F. Thompson (p.361), *'Physiological Psychology'*, Freemans, SF.

Scovel-Shinn, Florence (1928) *'Your Word is Your Wand'*

Shealy, Norman, and Myss,C., (1990*) The Creation of Health'*, Stillpoint, NH

Sisson, Colin *'Wounded Warriors'* Inner Adventures Publishing NZ,

Starhawk, (1994) *'The Fifth Sacred Thing'*, Bantam

Sutherland, W.G. , D.O. (1990) *'Teachings in the Science of Osteopathy'* (from writings in the 1940's) Rudra Press

Talbot, Michael (1992) *'The Holographic Universe'*, NY Harper Perennial.

Upledger, John, D.O.(1990) *'Somato-emotional release and beyond'*, Upledger Institute Publishers.

Upledger, J., D.O. (1991) *'Your Inner Physician and You'* UI Enterprises

Wall, P.D. and Melzack, R.(1989 2nd Ed.) *'Textbook of Pain'*, NY Churchill Livingstone.

Walsch, Neale Donald, (1996) *'Conversations With God'* Charlottesville, VA: Hampton Roads Pub.

Wilde, Stuart: (1984) *'The Force'*, Hay House

Wapnick, Kenneth : (2004) *'Ending Our Resistance To Love: A Practice Of A Course In Miracles'* – Foundation for Course in Miracles

Zukav, Gary (1989) *'The Seat of the Soul'* Simon and Schuster Fireside, NY

WEBSITES USED

'Wikipedia' – for dates and simple facts
On Electricity   http://www.eskimo.com/~billb/miscon/speed.html
          http://hyperphysics.phyastr.gsu.edu/Hbase/electric/watcir.html#c4

Michio Kaku , physicist http://www.mkaku.org

Deepak Chopra – on Jesus' 'Resist not evil'
http://www.intentblog.com/archives/2005/12/what_does_jesus

On 'Resist not evil'
http://www.swedenborgdigitallibrary.org/FHS/fhs38.htm

Prem Rawat's message
http://www.wordsofpeace.eu/en/index.php?Id=3
'
Starstuffs' - Physics & Consciousness:
http://www.starstuffs.com/physcon2

Parenting   http://www.naturalparenting.com.au

'Breatharian'- Jasmuheen   http://www.jasmuheen.com

Indigenous 'religion'   http://origin.org/ucs/sbcr/indigenous.cfm

Abraham-Hicks on consciousness   http://www.abraham-hicks.com
Sondra Ray, Rebirthing   http://www.sondraray.com

Artemis Theatre Co.   www.doorways2power.co.uk

David Lourie - get 'Dharma The Cat's 'Philosophy With Fur' at

http://www.DharmaTheCatCartoons.com

On Chaos and the Psyche www.schuelers.com/ChaosPsyche

Movies Recommended
'Spiritual movies' –   The Moses Code, The Celestine Prophecy
                                         The Secret, What the Bleep do we Know?
                                         Down the Rabbit-hole,   Peaceful Warrior
                                         Conversations with God *Heal Your Life*
                                         Powaqqatsi / Koyaanisqatsi / Naqoyqatsi /
                                         Baraka, Gandhi, The Power of One, Thunderheart
                                         The Green Mile, Whaleride,r Japanese Story,
                                         Over the Hill, Farinelli, Schindler's List,
                                         The Kite Runner, Finding Nemo,
                                         Groundhog Day, Life of Brian

With many thanks also to Hubble for their wonderful photograph of the Pinwheel
Galaxy used on the book cover, and all their beautiful photographs made
available in the public domain of their
NASA-linked website http://hubblesite.org

Please visit my website for updated information on the Book
and related workshops etc:- www.resistancejourneys.com
For a personal telephone consultation regarding issues high-lighted by this
book, please contact me through this Website.
There is also a pack of 'divination cards,' each one of which has inspiring
and unique artwork on the back, called "25 Universal Laws.' Please see the
website for further details

Other titles from MasterWorks International

Available from all good bookstores or direct from MasterWorks International. Please visit http://www.mwipublishing.com

Quinta-Essentia
by Morag Campbell

A study of the Five Elements of Ether, Air, Fire Water and Earth.

A Promise Kept
by Morag Campbell

Autobiographical account of a profound spiritual adventure set in England and ancient Hawaii.

The Art of Mental Wellbeing - The Polarity Of Mental Wellbeing and Mental Disorder beyond the Medical Approach
by Tony Caves

An exploration of sacred geometry and energy in relation to mental health.

The Power of Love - A Guide to Consciousness and Change
by Phil Young and Morag Campbell

The ancient Polynesian viewpoint on spiritual development retold for the modern world.

The Way of the FlameKeeeper
By David Kala Ka Lā

A no punches pulled account of spiritual journeying

Polarity Therapy - Healing with Life Energy
By Alan Siegel ND and Phil Young

A clear extensively illustrated instruction manual in this unique Healing Art.

Earthkind
by Morag Campbell

There is something for everyone in this light-hearted tale with a strong ecological message.

Lightning Source UK Ltd.
Milton Keynes UK
UKOW022038090212

187003UK00002B/14/P